AINSLEY'S BIG COOK OUT

Ainsley Harriott

This book is published to accompany the television series
Ainsley's Big Cook Out which was first broadcast in 1999.
The series was produced by BBC Birmingham.

Executive Producer: Roger Casstles
Producer: Sara Kozak
Directors: Lynda Maher and Micci Billinger
Assistant Producer: Sue Ashcroft

Published by BBC Worldwide Ltd,
80 Wood Lane, London W12 0TT

First published 1999
Reprinted 1999
© Ainsley Harriott 1999
The moral right of the author has been asserted.

ISBN 0 563 38489 1

Recipes developed and written in association with Silvana Franco
Studio photographs by Gus Filgate © BBC Worldwide Ltd 1999
Location photographs by Craig Easton © BBC Worldwide Ltd 1999

Commissioning Editor: Nicky Copeland
Project Editor: Sally Potter
Art Directors: Ellen Wheeler, Lisa Pettibone
Design by Town Group Creative
Food Stylist: Silvana Franco, assisted by Kate Jay
Props Stylist: Penny Markham

Set in Franklin Gothic
Printed and bound by Imprimerie Pollina s.a, France

Colour origination by Radstock Reproduction Ltd, Midsomer Norton
Jacket printed by Imprimerie Pollina s.a, France

CONTENTS

INTRODUCTION

Hello and welcome to *Ainsley's Big Cook Out!* It has given me enormous pleasure to write this book, especially as the activities required for both the television series and the book – travelling and barbecuing – are two of my favourite pastimes. I have been allowed to indulge in all sorts of wonderful aromas and exciting flavours, many of them captured while we were filming across the Americas. Now I can share them all with you – and you'll see as you flick through the book that you're in for a sizzling treat.

I've kept the recipes relatively simple and quick, yet in no way have I compromised on taste. There are flavours from Canada such as my Quidi Vidi fish cakes from Newfoundland and my Fire-glazed duck with plum dipping sauce from Quebec. Then on to Kansas City – land of the blues, booze and barbecues – where the barbecue sauce is thick, sweet and rich and the beans help cowboys keep their saddles warm. Appropriately enough, we travel next to the Windy City, Chicago, for a Deli pizza feast on the coals. Then Birmingham, Alabama, for a chicken Brummie balti, and off down to the Keys in sunny Florida for Jalapeño prawn ladders. From Oaxaca (pronounced '*wahaca*'), Mexico I've brought you Scorching salsa and Chilli-skin garlic-stuffed poussins. The Brazilian treats come in the form of Amazonian fish kebabs and Sizzling seafood rice from Bahia. And don't cry for me Argentina, especially after my Chicken empanadas with chimichurri (sounds like a song from *Mary Poppins*) or indeed my Heavenly herb-tied tuna. Believe me when I say this simply touches the surface of the fabulous range of dishes I experienced throughout the Americas.

Barbecuing is one of the easiest and oldest forms of cooking in the world. You can cook on just about anything. Many people spend a lifetime learning the art of barbecuing, and connoisseurs like to get the combination just right – lots of smoke, controlled heat and the right timing, often measured in half days rather than hours. Although this book does include a few recipes for the connoisseur, I've concentrated on dishes that are easy and extremely enjoyable to prepare.

Don't forget that barbecuing need not be restricted to summer days – you really can barbecue all year round. Even your Christmas turkey can be a barbecued treat if you're lucky enough to own a covered kettle barbecue, a hooded barbecue or a gas barbecue with a rotisserie. You'll also find that this book can easily be used indoors as well as out. Nearly all the recipes can be cooked in your kitchen: in your char-grill pan, under the grill, in a hot oven or even in a frying pan. This really is a book for all seasons. So, come on everybody, let's get smokin'.

AINSLEY'S KITCHEN TIPS

To help you on your way, here are a few guidelines on some of the cooking techniques referred to in the recipes.

To chop onions or shallots finely. Peel the onion, leaving the root end intact. Sit your onion root side down on a chopping board and thinly slice through the onion almost down to the root. The closer together you make the cuts, the finer your finished dice will be. Slice the onion in half through the middle cut, lay it flat side down on the board and thinly cut up towards the root again. Now slice across the onion and it will miraculously fall away in neat little pieces. Throw away the root end.

To peel garlic cloves. A nifty way of quickly getting the papery skin off the outside of a garlic clove is to place it on a board and very lightly crush it under the blade of a large kitchen knife. The skin will drop off just like magic.

To chop herbs. You can of course do this on a chopping board with a sharp knife, but a crafty little trick is to pack the herbs loosely in a coffee mug and chop around inside the mug with a pair of scissors until they are done to your liking.

To seed and chop a fresh chilli. Some people like to wear rubber gloves to do this job. If not, you have to be careful not to touch your eyes, mouth, etc. for a while afterwards. You can simply cut the chillies in half lengthways and then scoop out the seeds with a teaspoon so that you don't touch the seeds, which are the most fiery bits. Then you just need to chop the flesh finely. You can, of course, leave the seeds in if you like things extra hot.

To skin, seed and dice a tomato. Cover the tomato in boiling water and leave for 30 seconds. Drain, cover with cold water and, when cool enough to handle, peel off the skin. Cut the tomato into quarters, discard the seeds and finely chop the flesh.

To skin peppers. Place the whole, barbecued, roasted or grilled pepper in a plastic bag and close tightly. Alternatively, place in a heatproof bowl and cover with a clean tea towel – the steam created helps lift the skin away from the flesh. Set aside for 5 minutes or so. Holding the pepper over a bowl, pierce a hole in the bottom, then gently squeeze the pepper to let out all the juices that have gathered inside (stir these tasty juices into dressings and sauces). Peel off and discard the skin, then cut the pepper open and scrape out the seeds. Slice or dice the flesh as required.

To pare the rind off a lemon or lime. Thinly peel off the coloured part of the skin using a really sharp potato peeler, making sure you don't take off too much of the underlying bitter white pith with it.

To roast whole spices. Roasting brings out all the wonderful flavour of spices. Heat a dry, heavy-based frying pan over a high heat until it is really quite hot. Add the spices and shake the pan over the heat until they start to smell aromatic and have darkened very slightly. You can now either grind them up in a pestle and mortar or electric coffee grinder, or leave them whole.

To toast sesame seeds, pine kernels and other nuts. Spread them over a shallow baking tray, then slide them under a hot grill or into a hot oven and cook for a few minutes, shaking the tray every now and then, until they are lightly browned all over. Watch them like a hawk, though – they can burn in a matter of seconds.

To make fresh white breadcrumbs. Remove the crusts from slices of fresh white bread and whizz the remaining parts around in a food processor for a couple of minutes until they have broken down into crumbs.

Previous page: A quick kip before I get back to my barbecue (Mexico)

AINSLEY'S BARBECUING TIPS

To make dried breadcrumbs. Preheat the oven to gas mark 3, 160°C (325°F). Remove the crusts from the bread and whizz the remaining parts in a food processor to make fine crumbs. Tip the crumbs on to a baking sheet and place in the oven for 10–15 minutes, shaking the pan from time to time until the crumbs are crisp and dried – don't worry if they turn a little golden. Allow to cool (if you're a real perfectionist, you can sieve them to remove any large bits), then store in an airtight jar until ready to use. Remember that fresh white bread will yield roughly half its original weight in dried crumbs.

To sterilize bottles and jars. Wash them out in soapy hot water and rinse them thoroughly. Dry them in a warm oven set at gas mark 1, 140°C (275°F), then remove and leave to cool.

All the spoon measurements in this book are level unless otherwise stated. A tablespoon is 15 ml; a teaspoon is 5 ml.

Follow one set of measurements when preparing any of the recipes. Do not mix metric with imperial.

All the ingredients in the recipes are listed in order of use. This will make things easier for you when you are following the recipes.

The eggs used in the recipes are medium sized, unless otherwise stated.

Unless otherwise specified, pans can be placed on the barbecue rack in all recipes.

Do not leave raw food out in the sun before cooking. Keep it cool (but at room temperature) and covered until you are ready to cook it.

Lightly brush the cooking rack with a little oil before cooking. This should help prevent food from sticking to it.

Have a spray bottle of water handy to put out any flames as they appear.

Try to scrape most of the marinade off the food before grilling as this is what causes the coals to flare up during cooking.

Baste food with a sugary glaze only during the last 10 minutes or so of cooking, otherwise it tends to burn.

When cooking foil parcels of food, always use an extra-thick, heavy-duty foil.

Always soak bamboo and wooden skewers in water for about 30 minutes before using or they will catch fire during cooking.

Flat metal skewers for kebabs help to stop the food from spinning around as you turn them. A good trick is to thread the food on to pairs of parallel skewers which will hold it firmly in place.

Try not to pack food on to a skewer too tightly. Leave some gaps around each piece so that they can cook thoroughly.

A sturdy griddle pan can take the place of a barbecue for many of these recipes if you plan to bring your cooking indoors.

An oven pre-heated to gas mark 6, 200°C (400°F) can be used in place of a kettle barbecue, but cooking times may need to be adjusted accordingly.

Kebabs, steaks, chops and fillets of fish can all be cooked under a hot grill.

BARBECUE BASICS

MARINADES, RUBS & SAUCES

This section of the book contains stacks of ideas for flavouring your food, both before and after you've cooked it. Choose from tasty marinades to bathe your raw meat, fish, chicken and vegetables in, sticky glazes to brush on your food as it hits the heat, pungent South American-style dry rubs for meat and fish, as well as lots of salsas, sauces, relishes, flavour-packed mayonnaises and some super-speedy storecupboard dips.

The recipes in this section are ideal for livening up plain pieces of food, so try a little experimentation for some unexpectedly good results. Use the cooking chart (pages 26–27) as a guide to the cooking times and remember, once you feel confident, you can mix and match the recipes – for example, prawns flavoured with the Fragrant Thai marinade will be delicious served with the Sweet mean mango salsa. If you do need some help choosing what to serve with what, turn to the menu planners at the back of the book (pages 165–172) for a little extra guidance.

MARINADES

There is almost no better way of getting extra flavour into your food before you cook it than by using a marinade. And most marinades contain a tenderizing ingredient such as vinegar, citrus juice, wine or – in the Tandoori marinade – yogurt, and a blend of flavourings, so the benefits are three-fold: tenderization, extra flavour and added moisture. The following marinades are all quite low in oil, which will help minimize any flare-up while your food is cooking over hot coals.

Marinating is suitable not only for food destined for the barbecue, but also works well with any dish that is being cooked in a dry heat, which includes grilling, roasting and using a griddle pan.
- All these marinades are sufficient for 900 g (2 lb) of meat or fish.
- Make shallow cuts over the surface of the fish or meat before marinating if you wish. It will help the flavours to penetrate right into the food.
- Pour the marinade into a shallow, non-metallic dish, large enough to carry the food in one layer, and remember to give it a turn every now and then while it is marinating.
- Marinate red meats, poultry and game for 2 hours at room temperature or 24–48 hours in the fridge.
- Marinate fish, seafood and vegetables somewhere cool for 30 minutes or up to 2 hours in the fridge.
- Bring chilled foods back to room temperature before cooking.
- Never be tempted to re-use any left-over marinade on a fresh batch of meat or chicken as the risk of food poisoning is very high.

Moscow vodka marinade

This is really good on nice firm-fleshed fish such as salmon, monkfish and tuna. Remember not to marinade the fish for longer than an hour or two.

> 5 tablespoons vodka
> 3 tablespoons olive oil
> juice and grated rind of 1 lime
> 4 tablespoons chopped fresh dill
> 1 shallot, very finely chopped
> 1 tablespoon sugar
> 1 teaspoon salt

Mix all the ingredients together, then pour over the fish and marinate for 1 hour.

Soy-orange marinade

Great for pork and sausages.

> juice and grated rind of 1 large orange
> 1 tablespoon soy sauce
> 2 garlic cloves, crushed
> 1 tablespoon hot chilli sauce
> 2 tablespoons chopped fresh coriander

Mix all the ingredients together and use as required.

Previous page: Mmm, something smells real good. Must be my irresistible aftershave. Or is it my hot coals?

Fragrant Thai marinade

An aromatic marinade – best on fish or prawns.

2 garlic cloves, finely chopped
¼ teaspoon crushed chilli flakes
1 lemon grass stalk, finely chopped
2 cm (¾ in) piece root ginger, finely chopped
3 tablespoons fish sauce
juice of 3 limes
1 tablespoon sesame oil
2 tablespoons vegetable oil
1 tablespoon brown sugar

Mix all the ingredients together and use as required.

Tandoori marinade

This is particularly fantastic with chicken, but it also works remarkably well with thick white fish fillets such as cod or monkfish. It looks very bright when raw, but once the meat is cooked, it turns a lovely dark red.

1 x 150 g (5 oz) carton natural yogurt
1 garlic clove, crushed
1 teaspoon ground cumin
½ teaspoon cayenne pepper or chilli powder
pinch of ground turmeric
salt and freshly ground black pepper

Mix all the ingredients together and use as required.

Ooh-la-la red wine marinade

A simple French-style red wine marinade is marvellous on meat and chicken.

150 ml (5 fl oz) red wine
4 tablespoons caster sugar
2 tablespoons olive oil
1 teaspoon salt
1 red onion, finely chopped
4 garlic cloves, finely chopped
2 teaspoons herbes de Provence

Mix all the ingredients together and use as required.

Mexican marinade

Best on steaks and other cuts of beef.

1 tablespoon chilli powder
1 tablespoon paprika
½ teaspoon ground cumin
½ teaspoon dried oregano
2 teaspoons caster sugar
1 teaspoon salt
3 tablespoons tequila
juice of 1 lime
2 tablespoons olive oil
3 garlic cloves, finely chopped
2 tablespoons chopped fresh coriander

Mix all the ingredients together and use as required.

GLAZES

I love a sticky, shiny coating on my barbecued food and these simple sugar-based glazes give great results. The sugar slowly caramelizes over the heat to give the meat a deliciously rich, sticky finish. It's best to brush the glazes on half-way through or towards the end of cooking because they have a tendency to burn if you are not very careful. They are quick to prepare, so are generally best made up when you need them. All the following glazes are sufficient to coat 900 g (2 lb) of meat or poultry.

Sun honey-hoisin glaze

This deliciously sweet glaze is great with both chicken and pork.

2 tablespoons clear honey
2 tablespoons soy sauce
2 tablespoons hoisin sauce
1 tablespoon dry sherry
1 teaspoon freshly grated root ginger

Mix all the ingredients together, then brush on to the meat 10–15 minutes before the end of cooking.

Sweet rosemary glaze

Good with chicken and pork.

3 tablespoons caster sugar
4 tablespoons white wine vinegar
juice of 1 large orange
2 teaspoons chopped fresh rosemary
1 tablespoon olive oil
juice of ½ lime

Place the sugar, vinegar and orange juice in a small pan and boil rapidly for 5 minutes until reduced by half. Remove from the heat and stir in the rosemary, olive oil and lime juice.
Brush on to the meat 10–15 minutes before the end of cooking.

Sunset Caribbean meat glaze

This is a lovely glaze for meat – I particularly like to serve it with lamb.

100 g (4 oz) dark muscovado sugar
2 teaspoons English mustard powder
2 tablespoons rum
2 tablespoons olive oil
juice and grated rind of 1 lime

Mix together all the ingredients, then set aside for 10–15 minutes, stirring from time to time, until the sugar completely dissolves. Brush on to the meat 10–15 minutes before the end of cooking.

Sticky mango chutney glaze

Sweet, sticky and scrummy – I like it on duck.

3 tablespoons mango chutney
1 tablespoon orange marmalade
1 tablespoon Dijon mustard
1 teaspoon chilli sauce

Mix together all the ingredients, then brush on to the meat 10–15 minutes before the end of cooking.

Right: Devilish mint recado (page 14)

RECADOS & DRY RUBS

Recados are a type of dried, spiced mix or paste peculiar to Mexico and Brazil. They are usually pretty powerful owing to the inclusion of garlic and chillies, so tend not to be left on the meat for much over an hour. Meat marinated in a recado is commonly served with a salsa. A good example of this style of eating is Lynda's lazy lemon-rub steak with charred tomato salsa (page 82).

Dry rubs are particularly good on foods that are naturally quite high in fat, such as salmon and tuna, or steak and duck, as they draw some of the moisture out of the meat.

Pestle and pound garlic rub

This is very good on pork — try rubbing it into belly pork or pork shoulder before barbecuing.

  5 allspice berries
  5 garlic cloves
  1 tablespoon dried oregano
  1 tablespoon cumin seeds
  1 teaspoon salt
  1 teaspoon caster sugar
  1 teaspoon freshly ground black pepper

Using a pestle and mortar, pound all the ingredients together in a pestle and mortar to produce a dry paste. Marinate meat in the mixture for an hour, then barbecue.

Devilish mint recado

Great on seafood, especially firm white fish, such as cod.

  small bunch of fresh mint leaves
  small bunch of fresh coriander leaves
  2 garlic cloves
  1 small dried red chilli
  3 tablespoons olive oil
  1 teaspoon salt

Place all the ingredients in a liquidizer or food processor and whizz to make a rough paste. Brush on to the fish or chicken and leave to marinate for an hour or so before barbecuing.

Memphis rib rub

Rub it on your pork, then slap it straight on the barbie.

  2 teaspoons freshly ground black pepper
  1/2 teaspoon salt
  1 teaspoon caster sugar
  1 teaspoon onion salt
  1 teaspoon chilli powder
  1/2 teaspoon ground nutmeg
  1/2 teaspoon ground allspice
  2 garlic cloves, crushed

Mix all the ingredients together and cover until you are ready to use the rub.

Spiced and spiked chicken rub

Rubbing surely can't get any better than this. I like to rub this spicy mixture on to cubes of chicken thighs and then spear them on to skewers.

  1 tablespoon chilli powder
  1 tablespoon ground cinnamon
  1 teaspoon ground cumin
  1 teaspoon dried oregano
  1 teaspoon salt
  grated rind of 1 orange

Mix all the ingredients together, then rub into the chicken skin and flesh. Cover and chill for 3–6 hours before barbecuing.

Garlic-chilli recado

This is really quite pungent and should be left on the meat for 30 minutes and no more. I like it on red meat such as lamb chops or thick steaks.

  4 dried red chillies, such as bird's eye
  1 head of garlic, cloves separated and peeled
  2 teaspoons salt
  1 teaspoon dried oregano

Whizz all the ingredients together to form a paste. Chill until ready to use.

SALSAS

Versatile and colourful, the salsa has many valuable uses. Originating in Mexico, where it tends to be made with tomatoes and plenty of chilli, the salsa can come in many forms, but the word simply means sauce.

Generally a combination of finely diced vegetables or fruit with a good measure of fresh herbs, salsas can be cooked, but are often served raw; they can be either dry or pretty saucy. So, as you can see, there are no limits when it comes to salsa time. Serve them however you wish – spooned on to a piece of meat, fish or poultry, piled into a baked potato, spread on a sarnie or simply served with a bowl of crunchy tortilla chips.

Summery chilli chop salsa

It's very important that you stir the dressing ingredients into the peppers while they're still warm so that the flavour seeps into the flesh and all the juices really get a chance to mingle. Serve this with just about anything – fish, meat or vegetables. I love a dollop smeared on top of my melting cheese on toast!

SERVES 4
1 red pepper
1 yellow pepper
2 garlic cloves, finely chopped
1 red chilli, seeded and finely chopped
2 tablespoons chopped fresh parsley
2 tablespoons olive oil
2 teaspoons balsamic vinegar
salt and freshly ground black pepper

Barbecue or grill the peppers under a hot grill for 10–12 minutes, turning frequently until the skin is blackened and blistered. Place in a bowl, cover with a tea towel and leave for 5 minutes until the skins have softened.

Holding the peppers with a tea towel, pierce a hole in the bottom of each and squeeze the juices into a bowl. Skin, seed and dice the peppers, then add to the bowl of juices.

Stir in the garlic, chilli, parsley, olive oil and vinegar and season to taste. Leave at room temperature for a couple of hours or so before serving.

Salsa verde

Salsa verde is one of the most famous salsas and, as it just means 'green sauce', it's contents vary from place to place. Here's my delicious recipe – I like to serve it with barbecued fish, especially squid. The number of chillies you should use depends on your personal tolerance for chilli-heat.

SERVES 4
2–4 green chillies
8 spring onions
2 garlic cloves
50 g (2 oz) salted capers
1 sprig of fresh tarragon
1 bunch of fresh parsley
juice and grated rind of 1 lime
juice of 1 lemon
4 tablespoons olive oil
1 tablespoon green Tabasco
freshly ground black pepper

Halve the chillies and discard the seeds. Trim the spring onions and peel and halve the garlic cloves. Pulse briefly in a food processor until roughly chopped. Using your fingertips, wipe the excess salt off the capers, but don't rinse them in water. Add the capers to the food processor with the tarragon and parsley and pulse again until fairly finely chopped.

Transfer to a small bowl and stir in the lime juice and rind, lemon juice and olive oil. Stir the mixture loosely so the citrus juice and oil do not emulsify. Add green Tabasco and black pepper to taste.

Chill until ready to serve, but do not keep for more than 8 hours.

Sweet mean mango salsa

This is one of my all-time favourite salsas – the combination of sweet, juicy mango flesh with the hot, crunchy radish is a real winner.

SERVES 4
1 large, ripe mango, skinned, seeded and finely diced
12 radishes, finely diced
juice of 1 lime
1 tablespoon olive oil
2 tablespoons chopped fresh coriander
a few shakes of Tabasco
salt and freshly ground black pepper

Toss together the mango, radishes, lime juice, olive oil and coriander. Add Tabasco, salt and pepper to taste, then chill until ready to serve.

Maradona chimichurri

This a traditional Argentinian relish that is spooned over barbecued meats and served with Empanadas (page 87). Touched by the hand of God?

SERVES 6
1 onion, roughly chopped
1 green pepper, seeded and roughly chopped
1 tomato, roughly chopped
2 tablespoons fresh parsley leaves
2 garlic cloves, roughly chopped
5 tablespoons white wine vinegar
2 tablespoons olive oil
salt and freshly ground black pepper

Place the onion, green pepper, tomato, parsley and garlic in a liquidizer or food processor and whizz until finely chopped. Add the vinegar and oil, whizz again, then season to taste.
Before serving, chill for an hour or so.

Wicked kicking salsa

Habañero and Scotch bonnet chillies are truly fiery, so handle very carefully. Go on! It's got a wicked kick.

SERVES 6
1 habañero or Scotch bonnet chilli
2 ripe tomatoes, skinned, seeded and diced
2 mild green chillies, such as jalapeño, seeded and, finely chopped
2 tablespoons snipped fresh chives
2 tablespoons olive oil
1 tablespoon sherry vinegar
salt and freshly ground black pepper

Cook the habañero or Scotch bonnet chilli over very hot coals or hold in a gas flame for a couple of minutes, rolling frequently with a fork until the skin blisters. Place the chilli in a clean tea towel and rub it to remove the skin. Using a fork to hold the chilli, cut it open and scrape out the seeds. Finely chop the flesh.
Mix together the tomatoes, both types of chilli, the chives, olive oil and sherry vinegar. Season to taste, then set aside at room temperature for at least a couple of hours.

Potato passata wedge dip, back (page 23),
Sweet mean mango salsa, right and Japanese-style
cucumber and red onion relish, front (page 19)

FLAVOURED MAYONNAISES

Like salsas, flavoured mayonnaises make delicious dips for anything from a stick of celery to a hot, salted chip. They are also marvellous with any barbecued fish and most chicken or cheesey dishes. Use ready-made mayonnaise or follow the recipe for Garlic mayonnaise on page 99, excluding the four garlic cloves.

Angela's anchovy mayonnaise

My friend Angela knows her onions when it comes to having a bit on the side. Her mayonnaise is delicious served with all manner of things, including barbecued chicken and most kinds of barbecued meat and fish. Although it's not suitable for vegetarians, I particularly love it with the Butter bean burgers on page 94.

SERVES 4
4 anchovies
150 ml (5 fl oz) mayonnaise
1 garlic clove, crushed
freshly ground black pepper

Using a fork, mash the anchovies to form a paste. Stir into the mayonnaise with the garlic and a grinding of black pepper.

Crumbly blue cheese mayonnaise

Serve with melba toast or slices of fresh fruit.

SERVES 4
100 g (4 oz) blue cheese such as Roquefort or Stilton
150 ml (5 fl oz) mayonnaise
freshly ground black pepper
a dash of Tabasco

Crumble the cheese over the mayonnaise and gently fold in with the pepper and Tabasco. Chill until ready to serve.

Brazilian green mayonnaise

This is quite like a classic tartare sauce and is equally good with fish.

SERVES 4
2 salad onions, finely chopped
1 green chilli, seeded and finely chopped
1 tablespoon chopped fresh parsley
1 tablespoon snipped fresh chives
1 tablespoon chopped gherkin
1 hard-boiled egg, finely chopped
150 ml (5 fl oz) mayonnaise
juice of 1 lime

Stir together the salad onions, chilli, parsley, chives, gherkin, egg and mayonnaise. Squeeze in lime juice to taste, then chill until ready to serve.

Mashed mustard-garlic mayonnaise

This delicious 'mayonaise with a kick' really is the tops.

SERVES 4
1 head of garlic
1 tablespoon olive oil
150 ml (5 fl oz) mayonnaise
2 teaspoons grainy mustard

Halve the garlic bulb horizontally, place in a small roasting tin and drizzle with olive oil. Barbecue over medium coals or in a hot oven for 30 minutes until the garlic is tender.
Slip the cloves out of their papery skins and mash well. Stir into the mayonnaise with the mustard, then chill until ready to serve.

CHUTNEYS, PICKLES & RELISHES

Everyone loves a little pickle, the odd dab of chutney or a good dollop of relish. Here is a lovely selection, of which I hope one or two will become some of your favourites.

Wilmington's pickled watermelon rind

Now, this is most definitely the trendiest pickle going. It's a Southern American relish that's hitting all the latest London cafés and it really tastes great served with simple barbecued fish such as the Crusted chilli sprats on page 108.

After you've eaten the watermelon, cut back the rind so there are just a few millimetres of red flesh left on it. The rind actually weighs quite a lot, so about a quarter of an average-sized watermelon will yield enough rind to make this quantity of pickle.

MAKES 500 ML (17 FL OZ)
400 g (14 oz) watermelon rind
25 g (1 oz) salt
150 ml (5 fl oz) white wine vinegar
150 g (5 oz) caster sugar
1 teaspoon allspice berries
1 cinnamon stick
2.5 cm (1 in) piece root ginger

Carefully slice the green skin off the watermelon, then cut the rind into 1 cm (^{1}/$_2$ in) dice. Place the diced rind in a large bowl and sprinkle over the salt. Leave for 3–4 hours until the rind releases lots of water.
Place the vinegar, sugar, allspice, cinnamon and ginger in a pan and bring to the boil, stirring until the sugar dissolves.
Drain the watermelon rind and rinse well. Add to the vinegar mixture and cook for 30 minutes until the rind is tender. Pour the mixture into a jar, allow to cool, then store in the fridge for up to 2 weeks.

Chilli jam

This is always a winner. Once you've tried it, you'll be back for more – and it goes with absolutely anything.

SERVES 4
1–2 tablespoons sunflower oil
1 onion, finely chopped
2 garlic cloves, finely chopped
2 red chillies, seeded and finely chopped
juice of 1 orange
1 tablespoon clear honey
1 tablespoon malt vinegar
2 tablespoons tomato ketchup

Heat the oil in a small pan and cook the onion for 2–3 minutes. Add the garlic and chillies and cook for a further 2 minutes until softened. Stir in the orange juice, honey, vinegar and tomato ketchup and simmer gently for 5 minutes. Serve warm or cold.

Japanese-style cucumber and red onion relish

This Oriental relish is fresh, cool and crunchingly different. Try it with crispy chicken thigh brochettes (page 56) or Clare's Chinese crispy bubbled belly pork (page 72).

SERVES 6
1 large cucumber
2 small red onions, thinly sliced
3 tablespoons rice wine vinegar
^{1}/$_2$ teaspoon salt
^{1}/$_4$ teaspoon dried chilli flakes
2 tablespoons finely chopped fresh coriander

Using a swivel-style peeler, remove alternate strips of peel from the cucumber so that it is striped with green and white. Halve the cucumber lengthways and, using a teaspoon, scoop out and discard the seeds.
Thinly slice the cucumber diagonally and place in a large bowl with the red onion, vinegar, salt and chilli flakes and set aside for an hour or so until the vegetables have wilted.
Drain the relish to remove any excess liquid, then stir in the coriander. Chill until ready to serve.

Rich rhubarb chutney

This is a lovely, soft chutney that's especially nice served with fish.

MAKES 1 LITRE (1³/₄ PINTS)
1 kg (2¹/₄ lb) fresh rhubarb, cut into 1 cm (¹/₂ in) lengths
175 ml (6 fl oz) freshly squeezed orange juice
2 large onions, finely chopped
4 cm (1¹/₂ in) piece root ginger, finely chopped
600 ml (1 pint) malt vinegar
400 g (14 oz) soft brown sugar
1 teaspoon allspice berries
1 teaspoon cumin seeds
1 teaspoon salt
1 teaspoon freshly ground black pepper

Place all the ingredients in a large pan. Bring to the boil, then cover and simmer gently for 1¹/₂ hours. Pour into a kilner jar, seal and leave to cool. Store in the fridge for up to a couple of weeks after opening.
For prolonged storage: pack this chutney into a sterilized jar (see page 7) and store in a cool, dark place for at least a month. Once opened, keep in the fridge and eat within a couple of weeks.

Best beetroot relish

This is the ultimate relish for all you beetroot lovers. Try this with a plain grilled fillet of fish such as trout or plaice.

SERVES 4
2 beetroots
1 shallot, finely chopped
2 cm (³/₄ in) piece root ginger, finely chopped
1 tablespoon red wine vinegar
1 tablespoon caster sugar
¹/₂ teaspoon salt
1 tablespoon chopped fresh dill

Wrap the beetroots in foil and cook in the barbecue embers for 30 minutes–1 hour until tender. Place the shallot, ginger, vinegar, sugar and salt in a large bowl.
When the beetroot are cool enough to handle, peel and finely dice them. Add to the shallot mixture and leave to cool completely. Stir in the chopped dill and chill until ready to serve.

Right: After a days' barbecuing over the hot coals, I can finally relax with a long, cool beer. Cheers! (Birmingham, Alabama)

SAUCES

Grilled and barbecued food is cooked over a dry heat, so in some cases, a little sauce on the side can add extra moistness as well as a fresh burst of flavour to your dish. The sauces that require cooking can be made both indoors and out. For recommendations of what to serve them with, read the introduction to each dish and by all means try being a bit adventurous – you don't have to serve the cranberry sauce with turkey, you know; try serving it alongside the Molten taleggio fondue on page 36 or with the Olive paste and parmesan-crumbed cutlets on page 63.

Oriental barbecue sauce

A touch sticky, a touch sweet, but always saucy – oh, what a treat.

SERVES 4
3 tablespoons hoisin sauce
3 tablespoons ketchup
1 tablespoon rice wine vinegar
1 tablespoon soy sauce

Mix all the ingredients together and chill until required.

Ainsley's barbecue sauce

This is a great all-purpose sauce. Use it to marinate meats or serve it dolloped on top of burgers, sausages or plain barbecued chicken.

SERVES 6
1 tablespoon vegetable oil
1 small onion, finely chopped
2 garlic cloves, finely chopped
1 red chilli, seeded and finely chopped
4 tomatoes, roughly chopped
4 tablespoons ketchup
2 teaspoons English mustard
2 tablespoons molasses sugar
2 tablespoons cider vinegar
1 tablespoon soy sauce
1 teaspoon chopped fresh rosemary
salt and freshly ground black pepper

Heat the oil in a pan and cook the onion, garlic and chilli for 3–4 minutes until golden. Add the tomatoes, ketchup, mustard, sugar, vinegar, soy sauce and rosemary, then cover and cook gently for 30 minutes until thickened and pulpy. Season to taste.
If you wish, pass it through a sieve to make a smooth sauce, or leave it a little chunky, if you prefer.

All seasons cranberry sauce

I find this a delicious accompaniment for barbecued poultry, and frozen cranberries are now available all year round. You may need to alter the quantity of sugar added according to your own tastes and the tartness of the cranberries.

SERVES 6
225 g (8 oz) cranberries, thawed if frozen
100 g (4 oz) caster sugar
grated rind and juice of 1 orange
$1/4$ teaspoon ground ginger

Place all the ingredients in a small pan. Bring to the boil and simmer for 15 minutes until the berries have all popped and the sauce is thick and glossy. Serve warm or cold.

Creole grainy mustard sauce

This is delicious with strips of chicken or slathered on barbecued cheese toasties.

SERVES 4
1 garlic clove, crushed
2 tablespoons grainy mustard
3 tablespoons mayonnaise
1 teaspoon horseradish sauce
1 tablespoon white wine vinegar
2 tablespoons olive oil
salt and freshly ground black pepper

Mix together the garlic, mustard, mayonnaise, horseradish, vinegar and olive oil. Season to taste and chill until ready to serve.

Teasing taco sauce

A mouth-watering treat. This piquant sauce is delicious served with my Now now! refried beans (page 131) and crisp taco shells.

SERVES 4
1 tablespoon sunflower oil
1 small onion, finely chopped
2 garlic cloves, finely chopped
$1/2$ teaspoon cumin seeds
1 star anise
2 tomatoes, roughly chopped
2 tablespoons soy sauce
2 tablespoons clear honey
2 tablespoons wine vinegar
1 tablespoon chilli sauce
$1/2$ teaspoon salt

Heat the oil in a small pan and cook the onion and garlic with the cumin and star anise for 3–4 minutes until softened. Add the tomatoes and cook for a further 3–4 minutes.
Stir in the soy, honey, vinegar, chilli sauce and salt. Bring to the boil and simmer rapidly for 5–10 minutes until thickened and pulpy. Serve warm or cold.

STORECUPBOARD DIPS IN A FLASH

Oh, no! They're early! Quick, whip up a speedy dip to serve with nibbles and drinks – without losing your cool.

Potato passata wedge dip

Aside from, maybe, mayonnaise, this is the best dip a chip or barbecued potato wedge could ever dream of. At a real push a mixture of ketchup and horseradish makes a pretty decent dip too.

200 g (7 oz) passata or creamed tomatoes
2 teaspoons horseradish sauce
a dash of Tabasco
salt and freshly ground black pepper

Mix together the passata and horseradish sauce, season to taste with Tabasco, salt and pepper. Serve at once.

Light and spicy yogurt dip

Lovely with crudités or shards of crispy poppadom.

1 x 200 g (7 oz) carton Greek yogurt
1 teaspoon curry paste
1 tablespoon mango chutney

Mix all the ingredients together and serve.

Cheese and onion crisp dip

Serve it straight with plain, ready-salted crisps.

1 x 250 g (9 oz) carton mascarpone cheese
1 red onion, finely chopped
squeeze of lime juice
salt and freshly ground black pepper

Mix together the mascarpone and onion. Add lime juice and salt and pepper to taste.

Spicy crunchy nut dip

Wonderful with either fish or chicken kebabs.

4 tablespoons crunchy peanut butter
3–4 tablespoons boiling water
1 teaspoon Worcestershire sauce
dash of Tabasco
juice of $1/2$ lime

Spoon the peanut butter into a bowl, then mix in enough boiling water to make the mixture soft enough for dipping into. Season with Worcestershire sauce, Tabasco and a squeeze of lime juice.

Pesto whip dip

Great with those lovely vegetable crisps you can buy.

1 x 200 g (7 oz) carton Greek yogurt
2 tablespoons pesto sauce

Whip all the ingredients together and serve.

Overleaf: Barbecues, blues and booze in downtown Memphis

COOKING TIMES

This chart will give you an idea of how long it takes to cook most types of fish and meat on a barbecue. However, these timings are only approximate because they do not only depend on the thickness of the food (a 2.5 cm (1 in) thick piece of steak will take approximately the same time to cook through, whether it weighs 225 g (8 oz) or 450 g (1 lb)), but also on the heat of each individual barbecue, the distance of the rack from the coals and the weather (on a cold day things will take a little longer to cook).

When dealing with a large joint of meat, the easiest way of telling if it is done to your liking is to push a meat thermometer into the thickest part of the meat to register the internal temperature, so as well as approximate cooking times, I have given internal temperatures as well. As with all roasts, it is important to remove large joints of meat from the barbecue on to a board, cover tightly with a piece of foil and leave them to rest for 5–10 minutes before carving (during which time the internal temperature will rise by approximately another 10°C (25°F). Resting time allows the meat to relax and the juices, which have been bubbling up to the surface during cooking, to soak back down into the meat, making it more moist and tender.

All these timings are for foods cooked over a medium-hot barbecue using the direct method (see page 183) unless otherwise stated.

BEEF

With steaks, it is best to sear them first on each side and then continue to cook them to your liking.

2.5–4 cm (1–1$^1\!/_2$ in) thick rump or sirloin steaks
Rare: 3–4 minutes on each side

Medium: 5–6 minutes on each side

Well done: 7 minutes on each side

4–5 cm (1$^1\!/_2$–2 in) thick fillet steak medallions
Rare: 4–5 minutes on each side

Medium: 7–8 minutes on each side

Well done: 8–9 minutes on each side

large joints, cooked over indirect heat
(allow 18–20 minutes per 450 g (1 lb))
1 hour for a 1.25 kg (2$^3\!/_4$ lb) rolled sirloin or cook until the internal temperature is 65°C (150°F)

2.5–4 cm (1–1$^1\!/_2$ in) thick beefburgers
Rare: 3–4 minutes on each side

Medium: 5 minutes on each side

Well done: 6–7 minutes on each side

beef kebabs
5–10 minutes, turning regularly

CHICKEN

All chicken must be well cooked but not dried out. As a general rule, white breast meat will take less time to cook than the darker meat such as the thighs and drumsticks.

175 g (6 oz) boneless chicken breasts
7–8 minutes each side

175 g (6 oz) boneless thighs
4–5 minutes each side

275–300 g (10–11 oz) breasts on the bone
25 minutes, turning regularly

225 g (8 oz) drumsticks and thighs on the bone
15–20 minutes, turning regularly

250 g (9 oz) chicken quarters
25–30 minutes, turning regularly

750 g (1$^1\!/_2$ lb) chicken halves
35–40 minutes, turning regularly

450 g (1 lb) whole poussins
40 minutes or until the internal temperature reaches 85°C (185°F)

1.5 kg (3 lb) whole chickens, cooked over indirect heat
(allow 15 minutes per 450 g (1 lb), plus 15 minutes) 1 hour or until the internal temperature reaches 85°C (185°F)

large chicken wings
20–25 minutes, turning regularly

chicken kebabs
10 minutes, turning regularly

LAMB

All these timings are for medium-rare lamb. Decrease the timings slightly if you like your lamb really pink and increase it a little if you prefer it well done.

2.5 cm (1 in) thick loin lamb chops
6–7 minutes each side

175 g (6 oz) lamb fillets
4–5 minutes each side

4 cm (1 $\frac{1}{2}$ in) thick leg of lamb steaks
6–7 minutes each side

larger joints, cooked over indirect heat
(allow 20 minutes per 450 g (1 lb)
1 hour 10 minutes for a 1.5 kg (3$\frac{1}{2}$ lb) leg of lamb or cook until the internal temperature is 60°C (140°F)

lamb kebabs
10–15 minutes, turning regularly

FISH

As a general rule, allow 10 minutes per 2.5 cm (1 in) thickness of fish. Be very careful not to overcook it as it will dry out very quickly and become tasteless.

200–225 g (7–8 oz) fish steaks (about 2.5 cm (1 in) thick)
4–5 minutes each side

75–100 g (3–4 oz) fish fillets
1 $\frac{1}{2}$–3 minutes each side, depending on the thickness

275–350 g (10–12 oz) whole fish
6–7 minutes each side

1.5 kg (3 lb) large whole fish
12–15 minutes each side, or until the internal temperature reaches 50°C (125°F)

large, raw prawns
2–3 minutes each side

PORK

It is important that pork is well cooked but it is very easy to dry it out. These timings will give you well-done pork which is still juicy.

2–2.5 cm ($\frac{3}{4}$–1 in) thick boneless steaks
7–8 minutes each side

2.5 cm (1 in) thick chump or loin chops
8–10 minutes each side

450 g (1 lb) pork fillets
25 minutes, turning regularly

larger joints, cooked over indirect heat
(allow 25–30 minutes per 450 g (1 lb) plus 25 minutes)
1 $\frac{1}{4}$–1 $\frac{1}{2}$ hours for a 900 g (2 lb) boned and rolled loin of pork or cook until the internal temperature is 75°C (170°F)

pork kebabs
12–15 minutes, turning regularly

SAUSAGES

8–10 minutes, turning now and then

THE TOUCH TEST
Another simple way of testing meat for readiness is to press it lightly with your finger.
Rare: The meat will give easily and no juices will appear on the surface.
Medium: The meat will still be slightly springy but a few juices will be starting to appear on the surface.
Well done: The meat will be very firm to the touch and the surface will be covered with juices.

APPETIZERS

BARBIE BRUNCH
or breakfast

For those of you who like to use the barbecue on your hols, this is a great idea with sizzling results. Yes, a full English breakfast on the barbie – it can be done!

SERVES 4
4 x 10 cm (4 in) diameter field mushrooms
2—3 tablespoons olive oil
2 tomatoes, chopped
2 garlic cloves, finely chopped
2 tablespoons chopped fresh parsley
salt and freshly ground black pepper
8 rashers streaky bacon
12 quails' eggs
1 small ciabatta loaf

Cut the stalks out of the mushrooms and brush the caps with a little oil. Mix together the chopped tomatoes, garlic, parsley, 1 tablespoon of oil and plenty of seasoning. Divide the mixture between the mushroom caps and cook over medium coals for 2–3 minutes until beginning to soften.

Meanwhile, cook the bacon next to the mushrooms for 5 minutes until crispy and golden

Crack 3 quails' eggs into each mushroom cap and cook for 8–10 minutes until just set.

While the eggs are cooking, halve the ciabatta loaf horizontally and cut each half in 2 to give 4 even-sized pieces. Brush the soft side with a little oil and cook on the barbecue for about a minute on each side until crisp and golden.

Place the toasts cut side up on 4 plates and arrange the bacon on top. Settle an egg-filled mushroom cap in the centre of each and serve. Bloody Mary anyone?

Previous page: Outside the original recording place of rock king Elvis Presley – Sun Studios, Memphis, Tennessee. Ooh, Ainsley – name that tune!

MOUNTIES'
Canadian pancakes

While I was filming in Canada I served brunch to a couple of Mounties and this is what I cooked for them – and they loved it. The combination of bacon and maple syrup may sound odd, but it's a Canadian classic. The sweetness of the syrup really complements the saltiness of the bacon. If you like it sweet and salty, this one's for you...

SERVES 4
12 rashers smoked streaky bacon, cut widthways into
   thin strips
4 salad onions, finely chopped
150 ml (5 fl oz) maple syrup
orange wedges to serve

FOR THE BATTER
100 g (4 oz) plain flour
a pinch of salt
300 ml (10 fl oz) milk
1 egg, beaten
a knob of butter, melted

Sit a sturdy, non-stick baking sheet directly on the coals. Cook the bacon on it for 2–3 minutes, then add the salad onions and cook for a further minute or so until the bacon is crispy and golden.

Meanwhile, make the batter. In a large bowl, stir together the flour and salt, make a well in the centre, pour in the milk, egg and melted butter and whisk to make a smooth, thin batter.

Set aside three-quarters of the bacon mixture. Ladle a quarter of the batter over the remaining bacon to make a thin pancake and cook for 1 minute until golden. Carefully turn the pancake and cook the underside for 30 seconds. Drizzle over some maple syrup and roll up tightly. Repeat to make 4 pancakes.

Carefully transfer each pancake to a serving plate, drizzle over a little more syrup and serve warm with orange wedges.

SUCCULENT SEARED
scallops with coriander and garlic oil dressing

This was the first recipe I cooked at the beginning of my television series. I was on top of Signal Hill in Newfoundland with the most amazing icebergs drifting by in the Atlantic Ocean behind me. Well, you may not have quite the same setting as I did when you get your barbie out for this dish, but the chances are that yours will taste every bit as good as mine did, and, boy, did they taste good... And remember, if you buy scallops out of their shells, ask the fishmonger to give you the shells separately.

SERVES 4
4 tablespoons olive oil, plus extra for brushing
juice of 1 lemon
2 garlic cloves, finely chopped
2 tablespoons finely chopped fresh coriander
salt and freshly ground black pepper
12 fresh scallops, in their shells

Make the dressing by whisking together the olive oil, lemon juice, garlic, coriander and plenty of salt and pepper.
Holding the scallops flat side up, slide a blade between the shells. Keeping the blade as close to the inside of the top shell as possible slice the ligaments so the shells open. Snap off the top shells and remove and discard the black stomach sac and lacy grey edging around the scallops. Cut the scallops away from the bottom shell, then wash the scallops and the bottom shells thoroughly.
Lightly brush the scallops with a little oil and cook over hot coals or in a hot griddle pan for just 1 minute on each side until well browned.
Return the scallops to the clean bottom shells and drizzle over the dressing. Eat warm.

Succulent seared scallops with coriander
and garlic oil dressing

MEXICAN OYSTER
shooters

Okay, so there's no actual barbecuing going on here, but what a way to get a party swinging! Go on, I dare you!

Like a Bloody Mary, this also makes a great hangover cure – a perfect way to stop your head spinning the morning after the barbecue the night before.

SERVES 4
4 small oysters
4 tablespoons tequila
100 ml ($3^1/_2$ fl oz) tomato juice
1 lime
sea salt
a few drops of Tabasco
freshly ground black pepper

Carefully shuck each oyster by easing an oyster knife between the pointed end of the shells and gently twisting it until the shells part. Place the shelled oysters in 4 shot glasses.
Pour a tablespoon of tequila over each oyster and top up each glass with tomato juice.
Add a squeeze of lime, a pinch of salt, a few shakes of Tabasco and a quick twist of freshly ground black pepper.
Down in one! 'Oh, you are awful!'

PARMA FIRED FIGS
with goats' cheese filling

Use fully ripe, fragrant figs for this recipe. A true melt-in-the-mouth experience that adds a touch of passion to any barbie feast.

SERVES 4
4 ripe, black figs
75 g (3 oz) soft goats' cheese
freshly ground black pepper
4 sprigs of thyme
4 slices Parma ham

TO SERVE
rocket leaves
olive oil
rock salt

Cut a deep cross in the top of each fig, cutting right down to, but not through, the base.

Cut the goats' cheese into quarters. Open out the figs, slip a wedge of cheese into each, season with plenty of black pepper then close the figs back together. Place a thyme sprig on the side of each fig and wrap the Parma ham round each one, enclosing the thyme sprigs.

Cook over hot coals for 4–5 minutes, rolling the figs on their sides until the Parma ham is crispy and ruffled around the edges.

Arrange a small pile of rocket leaves in the centre of four serving plates and place a fig in the centre. Drizzle around a little olive oil and scatter over some rock salt and freshly ground black pepper.

MOLTEN TALEGGIO
fondue

I've used the Italian cheese Taleggio for this because it has a such a lovely flavour, but other soft-rind cheeses, such as Camembert and Brie, are equally good. It is far better to leave the cheese on the barbecue for too long rather than undercook it, as it is at its most delicious when totally runny with a crusty, golden layer on the bottom. Ooh, lovely!

SERVES 2
1 x 250 g whole Taleggio
1 small baguette, cubed (leave crust on)
selection of small pickles, such as sweet silverskin
   onions or cornichons

Place the Taleggio in a square of strong foil and loosely bring up the edges to enclose the cheese.
Cook over medium–hot coals a few inches from the edge of your barbie for at least 20 minutes until the cheese is completely melted.
Serve the cheese in the foil with the cubes of bread and pickles for dipping. Washes down nicely with a chilled bottle of Orvieto white wine.

Right: Parma fired figs with goats' cheese filling (page 35)
Left: Another smiling moment in the Mexican midday sun

SMOKED
pepper-berry oysters

If you've got a kettle-style barbecue, this recipe works a treat – you'll
need to use conventional charcoal or briquettes – but don't try it on a
gas barbecue. You can get whole allspice at most supermarkets now.

SERVES 4
50 g (2 oz) unsalted butter
2 tablespoons very finely chopped salad onions
12 oysters on the half shell
25 g (1 oz) allspice berries
25 g (1 oz) black peppercorns
fresh lime wedges to serve

Gently heat the butter and salad onions in a small pan just for a
minute or two until the butter begins to bubble and carefully spoon it
over the oysters.

Scatter the allspice berries and peppercorns over the hot coals
and, when they begin to smoke, quickly arrange the oysters on the
grill rack.

Cover the barbecue and cook the oysters in the allspice smoke for 2
minutes until just warmed through. Serve 3 per person, each plate
garnished with a wedge of lime for squeezing over.

JACQUELINE'S
scented seared squid

The secret to lovely, tender squid is not to overcook it – sear it quickly over very hot coals. Served with bruschetta and salad, this makes a gorgeous lunch. Says who? Says my sister Jacqueline.

Buy the squid tubes from a good fishmonger and get them cleaned, or buy them frozen from Chinese supermarkets.

SERVES 4
1 ripe mango, skinned, stoned and finely diced
1 small red onion, finely diced
2 tablespoons chopped fresh coriander
1 teaspoon fish sauce
1 tablespoon soy sauce
1 tablespoon olive oil, plus extra for brushing
juice of 1/2 lime
12 small squid tubes, thawed if frozen

TO SERVE
Aromatic charred bruschetta (page 136)
leafy green salad

Mix together the mango, red onion, coriander, fish sauce, soy sauce, olive oil and lime juice. Spoon the mixture into the squid tubes.
Thread the squid on to 4 skewers, pinning the open end closed. Brush lightly with oil, then cook over very hot coals or in a hot griddle pan for just 2 minutes on each side.
Serve with Aromatic charred bruschetta and plenty of salad.

SILVANA'S SIZZLING
snappy mussels

Mussels are usually poached or steamed, but they are delicious when cooked on the barbecue. The heat from the coals opens the shells and also produces an amazing aroma. Choose the largest mussels you can find and take care not to burn your fingers! My mate Silvana serves this with wedges of bread, such as Baked garlic and fennel flatbread (page 143), to mop up all the scrummy juices. Happy snapping!

SERVES 4
450 g (1 lb) mussels
15 g ($^1/_2$ oz) butter, melted
1 tablespoon olive oil
3 tablespoons freshly grated Parmesan
2 tablespoons chopped fresh parsley
2 garlic cloves, finely chopped
$^1/_2$ teaspoon coarsely ground black pepper

Wash the mussels thoroughly, scraping off any barnacles with a round-bladed knife and pulling out the gritty beards. Sharply tap any open mussels with the knife and discard any that don't close.

Scatter the mussels over a fine rack and set over hot coals for about 5 minutes, removing each mussel as it opens. Allow the mussels to cool slightly then snap the top shell off each, leaving the mussel still attached to the bottom shell.

Mix together the melted butter, olive oil, Parmesan, parsley, garlic and black pepper. Place a small amount (about $^1/_3$ of a teaspoon) on top of each mussel.

Return the half shells to the barbecue, ensuring they are level so that the melting juices stay inside the shells, and cook for a couple of minutes until sizzling. Eat immediately.

Right: Silvana's sizzling snappy mussels
Below: Dancing in the street – it's compulsory in Bahia, Brazil

JALAPEÑO
chilli-prawn ladders

I first made these in Key West overlooking the beautiful waters of the Gulf of Mexico. The locals were so impressed that their barbie bar now has them on its menu. Go on...get laddering.

I use jalapeño chillies for this because they have a delicate flavour and quite a mild heat. Try and get a variety of colours for this recipe – red, green and yellow.

SERVES 4
6 red jalapeño chillies
6 green jalapeño chillies
6 fresh basil leaves, finely shredded
2 cm (³/₄ in) piece fresh root ginger, finely chopped
salt and freshly ground black pepper
12 raw tiger prawns
a knob of butter
lemon or lime wedges to serve

Slit open the chillies from top to tail, taking care to leave the stalk intact. Scrape out the seeds. Divide the shredded basil and chopped ginger between the chillies and generously season inside.
Shell the prawns, leaving the shell section intact. Place a whole prawn inside each chilli, leaving the tail poking out of the pointed end. Smear a little butter on top of each prawn, then squeeze the chillies together to enclose the prawns.
Thread 3 chillies, alternating the colours, on to 2 short, parallel soaked bamboo skewers so that the chillies look like the rungs of a ladder. Repeat to make 4 ladders.
Cook the chillies over fairly hot coals for about 5 minutes, turning frequently until they are softened and a little charred, and the prawns are cooked through.
Serve with a wedge of lemon or lime and chilled beers. Delicious...

CRISPY SPRING ROLLS
on the coals

These delicious little crispy rolls are ideal as both starter or snack. If you can't get spring roll wrappers, this recipe will also work using filo pastry as a substitute.

SERVES 4
2–3 tablespoons vegetable oil
2 Chinese leaves, finely shredded
50 g (2 oz) canned waterchestnuts, finely chopped
1 large carrot, cut into matchsticks
75 g (3 oz) bean sprouts
2 salad onions, shredded
1 teaspoon five spice powder
$1/2$ teaspoon sugar
$1/2$ teaspoon salt
2 tablespoons hoisin sauce
12 spring roll wrappers
1 teaspoon cornflour mixed with a little water
soy sauce to serve

Heat 1 tablespoon of the oil in a large frying pan and stir-fry the Chinese leaves, waterchestnuts, carrot, beansprouts, salad onions and five spice over a high heat for 1–2 minutes until beginning to soften.

Stir in the sugar and hoisin sauce and remove from the heat; set aside to cool slightly.

Open out the spring roll wrappers and place a spoonful of the stir-fried vegetable mixture on each one. Roll, up tightly, tucking in the edges; brush the final edge with the slated cornflour, then press down well to seal.

Lightly brush the spring rolls with oil and cook over hot coals or shallow fry for 4–5 minutes, turning occasionally until crisp and golden. Serve with a little soy sauce for dipping and drizzling.

MAIN COURSES

POULTRY

ATCHAFALAYA
Cajun chicken

Take a trip down the Atchafalaya River in Cajun country and you'll come across this classic dish. It's a must for all you spicy Cajun connoisseurs. It's simply delicious.

I like to use a whole chicken cut into 8 pieces for this dish, but you can use a mixture of thighs and drumsticks if you prefer. For quick cooking cut 3–4 slits in the chicken pieces – these allow the sauce to penetrate and reduce cooking time by approximately 10 minutes. Try serving this with the Spicy lime-charred corn on the cob, page 122.

SERVES 4
150 ml (5 fl oz) chicken stock
250 ml (9 fl oz) tomato ketchup
100 g (4 oz) brown sugar
1 tablespoon hot chilli sauce
1 tablespoon soy sauce
1 tablespoon Worcestershire sauce
1 onion, finely chopped
4 garlic cloves, crushed
1 teaspoon paprika
2 teaspoons chilli flakes
2 tablespoons red wine vinegar
1 medium chicken, 1–1.2 kg (2$^1/_4$–2$^1/_2$ lb),
   cut into 8 pieces
2 tablespoons olive oil
chips to serve

To make the barbecue sauce place the chicken stock, tomato ketchup, sugar, chilli sauce, soy sauce, Worcestershire sauce, onion, garlic, paprika, chilli flakes and vinegar in a small pan and simmer together gently for 20 minutes.

Brush the chicken pieces with the oil, then spoon over half the barbecue sauce.

Cook over medium coals or under a pre-heated grill for 30–45 minutes, turning occasionally, until the chicken is dark, glossy and cooked through. Serve with a basket of freshly fried chips and the remaining sauce.

Previous page: Strolling through the surf on beautiful Arembepe Beach, Brazil. This is the life...

CHILLI-SKIN
garlic-stuffed poussins
(Oaxaca style)

Choose the heat of your hot pepper sauce by varying the type of chilli you use. I prefer a combination of milder jalapeño chillies and Thai birds' eye chillies but the truly brave can always throw in the odd habañero or Scotch bonnet. As this recipe uses so many chillies, I've named it after the idyllic Mexican town of Oaxaca where the chillies are plentiful.

This recipe works best if you have a covered, kettle-style barbecue which acts more like an oven – if you have an open barbecue, you should spatchcock the poussins (see Spatchcocked spiced and spliced chicken page 55, for details) and serve the garlic and onion stuffing on the side.

SERVES 2
2 x 500 g (1 lb 2 oz) poussins (baby chickens)
Rosemaried sweet potato parcels to serve (page 128)

FOR THE STUFFING
1 head of garlic
1 red onion, cut into 8 wedges
1 lime, cut into 6 wedges
2 bay leaves
salt and freshly ground black pepper
2 tablespoons olive oil

FOR THE HOT PEPPER SAUCE
6 red chillies, seeded and roughly chopped
2 tablespoons red wine vinegar
3 tablespoons olive oil
1 small onion, roughly chopped
2.5 cm (1 in) piece fresh root ginger, finely chopped

To make the stuffing, halve the head of garlic horizontally and place in a small roasting tin with the red onion, lime wedges and bay leaves. Season generously, drizzle with olive oil and cook over medium-hot coals for 30 minutes until softened and a little charred.

Meanwhile, make the hot pepper sauce. Soak the chopped chillies in the vinegar for 5 minutes–1 hour, the longer the better. Heat the olive oil in a small frying pan and cook the onion for 7–8 minutes until softened and golden. Strain the chillies, reserving the vinegar, and add to the pan with the ginger. Cook for a further 3–4 minutes until the chillies are softened. Place the chilli mixture in a food processor and blend, or grind with a pestle and mortar to make a coarse paste. Gradually add the reserved vinegar then season to taste.

Lift the flap of skin at the back of the poussin breasts and gradually loosen the skin using your fingers. Spread a couple of teaspoons of the chilli paste under the skin of each bird then stuff the front cavities with the roasted vegetables. Cook in a kettle barbecue for 40 minutes, turning from time to time until cooked through and golden brown.

Serve with the remaining hot pepper sauce and the Rosemaried sweet potato parcels.

ALABAMA CHICKEN
Brummie balti

During the series I paid a visit to Birmingham, Alabama – I thought it might be fun to cook them our Birmingham's most famous dish – the balti. And boy, did they love it... I could probably run for mayor, it got that many votes of approval.

SERVES 4

4 boneless, skinless chicken breasts, quartered
2 tablespoons vegetable oil
1/2 teaspoon chilli powder
1/2 teaspoon turmeric
salt and freshly ground black pepper
1 onion, finely chopped
4 garlic cloves, finely chopped
4 cm (1 1/2 in) piece root ginger, finely chopped
6 tomatoes, roughly chopped
150 ml (5 fl oz) chicken stock
4 tablespoons balti curry paste
1 x 400 g (14 oz) can chick peas, drained

4 naan breads (see my Table-top naans, page 139)
2–3 tablespoons double cream
2 tablespoons chopped fresh coriander
lemon wedges to serve

Brush the chicken with a little oil, then dust with chilli powder and turmeric and season with salt and pepper. Cook over medium coals or in a large frying pan for 3–4 minutes on each side until well browned.

Meanwhile, heat the remaining oil in a balti pan or wok and stir-fry the onion, garlic and ginger for 3–4 minutes until golden. Add the tomatoes, cook for a couple of minutes until they begin to soften, then stir in the stock, curry paste and chick peas.

Add the chicken pieces to the pan and simmer together for 5–8 minutes until the chicken is cooked through.

Briefly warm the naan breads over the barbecue or under a hot grill.

Stir the cream and coriander into the balti and check the seasoning. Divide between serving bowls and serve with lemon wedges and the warm naan.

Below: The Amazonian rainforest is the biggest in the world – now, which way did the others go?

Right: Happy Cancun chicken chompers (page 50)

HAPPY CANCUN
chicken chompers

These yummy little sticks always go down well at parties. You can prepare the chicken at least 8 hours in advance if you want. For convenience you might want to buy packets of mini chicken fillets instead of breast. The delicious chilli dipping sauce is the perfect accompaniment, so you might need to make extra. Happy chomping!

SERVES 4

4 x 75–100 g (3–4 oz) skinless, boneless
  chicken breasts
rice noodles or plain boiled rice to serve

FOR THE MARINADE

1 teaspoon black peppercorns
4 garlic cloves
2 tablespoons fresh coriander leaves, plus extra,
  to garnish
1 teaspoon caster sugar
juice of 1 lime
1 teaspoon fish sauce
1 teaspoon light soy sauce
2 teaspoons sunflower oil

FOR THE DIPPING SAUCE

75 ml (3 fl oz) red wine vinegar
75 g (3 oz) caster sugar
2 chillies, seeded and finely chopped
$1/4$ teaspoon salt

Using a pestle and mortar, grind the peppercorns, garlic and coriander to make a paste. Then mix in the sugar, lime juice, fish sauce, soy sauce and sunflower oil until well blended.

Halve each chicken breast horizontally. Bat each piece out with a rolling pin until 5 mm ($1/4$ in) thick. Cut each piece lengthways into 3 cm (1 $1/4$ in) wide strips. Add to the marinade and set aside for about 1 hour.

Meanwhile, make the dipping sauce. Heat the vinegar and sugar together in a small pan, stirring until dissolved. Bring to the boil and simmer for 3–4 minutes, then remove from the heat, stir in the chillies and salt and allow to cool.

Thread the chicken strips on to soaked bamboo skewers and cook over hot coals for 4–5 minutes on each side until cooked through and well browned. Serve with rice noodles or plain boiled rice.

STORMING
Louisiana chicken and sausage gumbo

A classic gumbo always contains equal quantities of chopped pepper, celery and onion, known in Louisiana as 'the trinity'. I start with one large green pepper and then chop enough celery and onion to match it in volume.

The other key to an authentic gumbo is the roux, and in Louisiana it's cooked slowly over a long period of time until quite dark; this gives the gumbo its colour and lovely nutty flavour. And the last essential element of any true gumbo is okra, otherwise known as ladies' fingers.

Now you have all the basics behind you, go cook up a storm!

SERVES 4–6
4 tablespoons sunflower oil
50 g (2 oz) plain flour
4 boneless chicken thighs, halved
2 x 75–100 g (3–4 oz) boneless chicken
   breasts, quartered
2 tablespoons Cajun seasoning
4 chorizo sausages, weighing in total
   about 250 g (9 oz)
1 litre (1 3/4 pints) chicken stock
the trinity (see introduction above), roughly 1/2 lb
   each of chopped green pepper, celery and onion
3 garlic cloves, finely chopped
175 g (6 oz) okra, thinly sliced
salt and freshly ground black pepper
2 tablespoons chopped fresh parsley
boiled white rice to serve

To make the roux heat the oil in a large pan. Add the flour and cook gently for 10–15 minutes until the flour is chestnut brown.

Meanwhile, toss the chicken pieces in the Cajun seasoning and cook over the coals or in a griddle pan for 5 minutes on each side; set aside.

Halve the chorizos lengthways and cook over the coals or in a griddle pan, cut side down, for 2–3 minutes until crisp and lightly browned. Cut each half into slices 1 cm (1/2 in) thick, then set aside with the chicken.

When the roux is ready, slowly beat in the chicken stock. Add the chicken and sausage pieces, the trinity (green pepper, celery and onion), garlic and okra and bring to the boil. Cover and simmer for 1 hour, stirring occasionally, until all the vegetables are tender and the gumbo is nice and thick.

Skim off any fat from the top of the gumbo and season to taste. Stir in the parsley and serve with the rice. Simply and satisfyingly delicious.

CRISPY CHICKEN-
thigh brochettes

Brochette is just a fancy name for a kebab, and these juicy skewers
well deserve a snazzy title.

SERVES 4
8 boneless chicken thighs
16 fresh sage leaves
2 small red onions, each cut into 8 wedges
3 tablespoons olive oil
1 teaspoon balsamic vinegar
2 garlic cloves, crushed
$1/2$ teaspoon dried chilli flakes
salt and freshly ground black pepper

TO SERVE
salad leaves
Aromatic charred bruschetta (page 136)

Quarter each chicken thigh and thread, skin side out, on to 8 metal
skewers, alternating each piece with a sage leaf or red onion wedge.
Whisk together the olive oil, balsamic vinegar, garlic, chilli flakes and
plenty of salt and pepper. Brush the mixture over the brochettes and
cook over medium-low coals or under a pre-heated grill for 20–30
minutes, turning occasionally, until the chicken is crusty and dark
golden and the red onions are sweet and softened.
Serve on a bed of salad leaves with Aromatic charred
bruschetta.

**Right: Monkeying around in the
Amazon rainforest with my new
Brazilian friend, Woolly**

MOO POPS
sticky finger drumsticks

My children love this one, which is why I've named it after my daughter Madeleine (Moo Pops for short) – the glaze is so sticky that you can't eat the drummers without getting it all over your face. A mild to medium-hot chilli is good, but if you like it hot hot hot, I'm sure you'll know exactly what to do, you devil!

SERVES 4
4 tomatoes, seeded and roughly chopped
2 garlic cloves, finely chopped
1 red chilli, seeded and finely chopped, or pinch of
  dried chillies
2 cm ($^3/_4$ in) piece of root ginger, finely chopped
  or grated
2 tablespoons clear honey
2 tablespoons dark soy sauce
1 tablespoon malt vinegar
1 teaspoon salt
1 teaspoon Chinese five-spice powder
12 chicken drumsticks

Place the tomatoes in a small pan with the garlic, chilli and ginger and cook gently for 5 minutes until the tomatoes are pulpy.
Stir in the honey, soy, vinegar, salt and five-spice powder and cook for a further 5 minutes until well blended.
Deeply score the drumsticks and brush with the glaze. Barbecue over medium coals or under a pre-heated grill for 25 minutes, turning occasionally and brushing with the glaze until shiny and cooked through.

BLACKENED CHICKEN
Chichen-Itzá

A classic barbecue dish, probably as old as the famous ancient pyramid of Chichen-Itzá in southern Mexico.

I really like this recipe because the dry rub on the skin of the chicken blackens to a tasty, crunchy coating during cooking, leaving the flesh inside moist and juicy. How do you like yours?

SERVES 4
2 garlic cloves, crushed
1 tablespoon freshly ground black pepper
1 teaspoon dried oregano
1 teaspoon dried thyme
1 tablespoon paprika
1 tablespoon caster sugar
2 teaspoons chilli flakes
1 teaspoon English mustard powder
1 teaspoon salt
1 medium chicken, 1–1.2 kg
  ($2^1/_4$–$2^1/_2$ lb), quartered

TO SERVE
salad
fried potatoes

Mix the garlic, pepper, oregano, thyme, paprika, sugar, chilli, mustard powder and salt together in a large shallow dish. Roll the chicken quarters in the spice mixture and leave for 5–10 minutes.
Cook the chicken over medium coals for 30–45 minutes, turning occasionally, until the skin is blackened and the chicken is cooked through.
Serve with salad and fried potatoes.

SPATCHCOCKED
spiced and spliced chicken

Dishes such as this are very popular in Brazil. I like to serve it with Double dip spicy chips (page 126) and a big dollop of Brazilian green mayonnaise (page 18).

SERVES 4
1 medium chicken, 1–1.2 kg (2 $1/4$–2 $1/2$ lb)

FOR THE MARINADE
2 garlic cloves
2 red jalapeño chillies, seeded and roughly chopped
juice of 3 limes
$1/2$ teaspoon paprika
$1/4$ teaspoon Angostura bitters
$1/2$ teaspoon salt

Using a pestle and mortar, grind the garlic and chillies together to make a coarse paste. Transfer the paste to a large non-metallic dish and stir in the lime juice, paprika, bitters and salt.
Spatchcock the chicken: using a sharp kitchen knife, cut down either side of the chicken's breastbone and discard. Pull the chicken open and press it out flat. Push 2 metal skewers diagonally through the bird in a large cross shape to hold it flat.
Place the chicken in the spiced marinade, turning to ensure it's coated. Chill overnight.
Cook the chicken over medium coals or under pre-heated grill for an hour or so, turning occasionally, until the flesh is cooked and the skin crisp. Transfer to a large platter and cut into pieces at the table.

MUSTARD-MARJORAM
crust-bust chicken breasts

Spreading a paste such as this under the skin of chicken before barbecuing it is a really good way of adding flavour to the meat. Sun-dried tomato paste or even pesto can be used in the same way.

SERVES 4
2 teaspoons fresh marjoram leaves, finely chopped
1 tablespoon Dijon mustard
2 garlic cloves, crushed
grated rind of 1 lemon
salt and freshly ground black pepper
4 x 75–100 g (3–4 oz) part-boned chicken
   breasts, skin on

TO SERVE
salad
Charred tasty tatties (page 122)

Mix together the marjoram, mustard, garlic and lemon rind; season generously.
Gently loosen the chicken skin and spread the mustard mixture between the skin and flesh. Pull the skin back over the chicken to cover the mixture.
Cook over medium coals, skin side down first, for 20–30 minutes until crisp, golden and cooked through. Turn the chicken pieces once, a few minutes before the end of the cooking time. Remember those meat juices should run clear – that tells you the chicken's ready to tuck into. Serve with salad or my Charred tasty tatties.

JIM'S FIRE-GLAZED
duck with fresh plum dipping sauce

This oriental-style duck is delicious served with the fresh plum sauce. I cooked this in Canada using Quebec duck, which is particularly fatty. If the duck you use has a very thick layer of fat on it, cut it back so it's under 5 mm ($1/4$ in) thick.

If you don't have any plums, nectarines make a surprisingly good substitute. But Jim 'The Fixer' prefers plums.

SERVES 4
4 x 150–175g (5–6 oz) boneless duck breasts

FOR THE MARINADE
3 tablespoons maple syrup or clear honey
2 tablespoons soy sauce
1 teaspoon Chinese five-spice powder

FOR THE DIPPING SAUCE
450 g (1 lb) halved and stoned plums or damsons
1 cinnamon stick, halved
150 ml (5 fl oz) white wine
1 bay leaf
1 tablespoon wine vinegar
2–3 tablespoons light muscovado sugar
salt and freshly ground black pepper

In a shallow bowl, mix together the syrup, soy sauce and Chinese five-spice powder. Deeply score the duck skin and add to the marinade, turning to coat it, then set aside for 5 minutes.
Place the plums, cinnamon stick, wine and bay leaf in a small pan set over the coals. Simmer gently for 30 minutes until the plums are completely softened.
Meanwhile, cook the duck, skin side down, first for 8–10 minutes on each side until well browned but still a little pink in the centre; set aside to rest for 5 minutes.
Sieve the sauce and stir in the vinegar, plus sugar, salt and pepper to taste. Spoon into small serving bowls. Carve the duck diagonally and serve with the warm dipping sauce. It's finger-lickin' good.

Jim's fire-glazed duck with fresh plum dipping sauce

LAMB

CHILLI AND MUSTARD
crusted leg of lamb

Save time on marinating your meat – just rub on this mustard mix and let it crust up over the coals.

This recipe uses butterflied leg of lamb, which has had its bone removed and then been opened flat. It's easy enough to do it yourself but a lot easier to ask your butcher to do it for you.

This is fabulous served with the Charred couscous pepper cups on page 114.

SERVES 10
3 tablespoons Dijon mustard
1 tablespoon plain flour
1 tablespoon soy sauce
1 tablespoon hot chilli sauce
1 tablespoon olive oil
2 teaspoons finely chopped fresh rosemary
$1/2$ teaspoon salt
$1/2$ teaspoon freshly ground black pepper
2 kg (4 $1/2$ lb) butterflied leg of lamb

Mix together the mustard, flour, soy sauce, chilli sauce, olive oil, rosemary, salt and pepper to make a smooth, thick paste.
Smear the paste all over the lamb, then cook over medium coals for 40 minutes, turning every 10–15 minutes until crusty and browned on the surface but still a little pink in the centre.

OOZING OSORIO
stuffed lamb

Near Porto Alegre in Brazil is a town called Osorio. The restaurants here serve highly flavoured fish and meat, often tied up with herbs, which have been roasted over the coals. The smells are wonderful. Hopefully, I've captured some of these aromas and flavours in this beautiful lamb recipe. A lovely way to stuff, cook and eat juicy lamb.

SERVES 4
4 x 75–100 g (3–4 oz) lamb neck fillets
2 tablespoons sun-dried tomato paste
100 g (4 oz) mozzarella, thinly sliced into strips
12 bay leaves
oil for brushing
rock salt and freshly ground black pepper

TO SERVE
green salad
crusty garlic bread

Cut the lamb fillets open lengthways taking care not to cut right through. Spread the inside of the meat with sun-dried tomato paste and arrange the mozzarella on top.
Fold the lamb fillets back together and place 3 bay leaves down the length of each.
Tie the lamb in several places with string, then brush with oil, season and cook over hot coals for 10–12 minutes, turning frequently until well browned.
Allow the meat to rest for 5 minutes, then carve at an angle into thick slices and serve with plenty of crunchy green salad and warm crusty garlic bread.

YUSEF'S
Yucatan lamb

A classic dish from the Yucatan region of Mexico. You can actually get something very similar to this dish from one of the many local restaurants in the area, although the strong chilli presence is enough to blow your head off. But you can trust Ainsley – this version, my nephew Yusef's favourite, is wonderful.

I've used shoulder of lamb, but if you wish you can use leg. It's a more expensive cut, but is less fatty and should be cooked for about 30–45 minutes.

SERVES 4
4 unpeeled garlic cloves
1.5 kg (3 lb) boneless shoulder of lamb, cubed
2 large tomatoes, diced
3 tablespoons malt vinegar
2 teaspoons chilli powder
2 teaspoons brown sugar
1 tablespoon paprika
1 teaspoon dried oregano
$1/2$ teaspoon dried thyme
$1/2$ teaspoon salt
$1/2$ teaspoon freshly ground black pepper

TO SERVE
warm tortillas
shredded salad

Cook the garlic cloves on a rack set over hot coals for 5 minutes, turning frequently until lightly charred.
Place the lamb and tomatoes in a large bowl. In another, smaller bowl, mix together the vinegar, chilli powder, sugar, paprika, oregano, thyme, salt and pepper. Peel the garlic cloves and crush them into the spice mixture. Add the spice mixture to the meat and tomatoes and toss together well.
Divide the mixture between 4 large, extra-strong squares of foil and scrunch the edges together at the top. Cook over medium-hot coals for about 1 $1/2$ hours, shaking the parcels from time to time, until the meat is tender and succulent.
Give each diner a parcel to open out at the table and serve with warm tortillas and shredded salad.

SPICED MAZATLÁN
meatballs

These delicious, moist little meatballs, delicately flavoured with spices from the Middle East, taste brilliant topped with yogurt and red onion and rolled up in soft, warm flatbread. In Mexico, they serve very similar meatballs called *albondigas*, which are barbecued or fried, then smothered in taco sauce (see mine on page 23) and cooked in a hot oven for 5 minutes or so, until bubbling – yummy...

SERVES 4
500 g (1 lb 2 oz) lean minced lamb
a pinch of salt
1 onion, finely chopped
2 teaspoons ground cumin
1 teaspoon ground allspice
$1/4$ teaspoon cayenne pepper
4 tablespoons roughly chopped fresh coriander

TO SERVE
4 Middle Eastern flatbreads or plain naan
1 red onion, thinly sliced
1 x 200 g (7 fl oz) carton Greek yogurt
1 lemon, cut into wedges

Place the lamb, salt, onion, cumin, allspice, cayenne and coriander in a food processor and whizz until well blended. Using wet hands, shape the mixture into 20 meatballs and cook over hot coals or in a non-stick frying pan for 10 minutes, turning frequently until well browned.
Warm the flatbreads for 1–2 minutes on each side until softened and warmed through.
Scatter the red onion over the flatbreads and spoon a dollop of Greek yogurt on each. Arrange the meatballs on top, then roll into a cone shape. Serve each with a lemon wedge.

Spiced Mazatlán meatballs

LEMON LAMB LIVER
skewers

Liver is fantastic cooked on a barbecue – it develops a lovely crust but stays tender and a little pink in the centre, just the way I like it! Try it with Saffron-scented rice (page 130) and a crisp green salad.

SERVES 4
4 garlic cloves, crushed
3 tablespoons olive oil
1 tablespoon chopped fresh mint
salt and freshly ground black pepper
500 (1 lb 2 oz) lamb's liver, cut into slices 1 cm ($1/2$ in) thick
2 lemons, each cut into 8 wedges
green salad to serve

Mix together the garlic, olive oil, mint and plenty of salt and pepper. Cut the liver into chunks and place in a shallow dish. Pour over the garlic mixture and set aside for 1–2 hours.
Thread the liver pieces on to 8 skewers, finishing with a lemon wedge. Cook over the hot coals for 4–5 minutes, turning occasionally, until good and crusty on the outside.
Serve with piles of green salad and extra lemon wedges for squeezing over the liver skewers.

OLIVE PASTE
and Parmesan-crumbed cutlets

The beauty of this recipe is that you can cook it either on a barbecue (make sure the rack is not too widely spaced) or indoors in a frying pan with a little olive oil and foaming butter. Either way it's simply and totally scrumptious.

SERVES 4

12 lamb chops
salt and freshly ground black pepper
2 tablespoons black olive paste
2 tablespoons seasoned flour
2 eggs, beaten
1 tablespoon snipped fresh chives
8 tablespoons dried natural breadcrumbs
1 tablespoon freshly grated Parmesan
oil for brushing
mixed salad to serve, such as Syd's chicory, blue cheese
   and walnut salad (page 132)

Season the chops with salt and pepper. Thinly spread the black olive paste on both sides, then dust very lightly with seasoned flour.
Whisk together the eggs, chives and a little seasoning. In a separate shallow dish, mix together the breadcrumbs and Parmesan.
Dip the floured chops in the beaten egg, then coat well in the breadcrumb mixture, gently shaking off any excess crumbs.
Brush the barbecue rack with a little oil and cook the chops over medium-hot coals for 5 minutes on each side until crunchy and golden but still a little pink in the centre. Serve with a mixed salad, such as Syd's chicory, blue cheese and walnut salad.

WHIZZ AND DRIZZLE
lamb tattie towers

The combination of barbecued peppers, potatoes and tender pink lamb drizzled with a really scrumptious dressing will instantly become a party favourite. A bottle of Cabernet Sauvignon helps it along its way nicely.

SERVES 4
2 large potatoes, cut into 1 cm ($^1/_2$ in) thick slices
1 large red pepper, quartered and seeded
1 yellow pepper, quartered and seeded
olive oil for brushing
salt and freshly ground black pepper
8 lamb noisettes or small lamb chops
salad leaves to serve

FOR THE DRESSING
1 small garlic clove
25 g (1 oz) pitted black olives
1 teaspoon fresh rosemary leaves
1 tablespoon roughly chopped fresh parsley
1 tablespoon freshly grated Parmesan
juice of 1 lime
4 tablespoons olive oil

Brush the potatoes and peppers with olive oil, season and cook over medium coals or in a griddle pan for 8 minutes on each side until tender and golden.

Brush the lamb with oil, season and cook for 4–5 minutes on each side until well browned but still a little pink in the centre.

Meanwhile, make the dressing: place the garlic, olives, rosemary and parsley in a food processor and whizz until well blended. Add the Parmesan, lime juice and olive oil and whizz again until well blended; season to taste.

Pile the potatoes, peppers and lamb noisettes high on 4 serving plates. Drizzle over the dressing and serve warm with salad leaves.

Whizz and drizzle lamb tattie towers

PORK

DODG'EM
and down'em cowboy ribs

I made these in Dodge City, USA, dressed up just like the outlaw Jesse James. Yes, I felt like a right old jesse, but the ribs were a knock-out as you'll discover.

The beer marinade used in this delicious dish tenderizes the meat, making for really juicy ribs.

SERVES 4
1 x 330 ml (11 1/2 fl oz) bottle strong lager
grated rind and juice of 1 lime
2 garlic cloves, crushed
2 teaspoons chopped fresh thyme
2 tablespoons dark muscovado sugar
1 hot, smoked chilli (e.g. chipotle), crushed, or 1 teaspoon chilli flakes
salt and freshly ground black pepper
1 sheet pork ribs (about 750 g/1 1/2 lb)

Mix together the beer, lime rind and juice, garlic, thyme, sugar, chilli and plenty of seasoning.
Add the ribs to the beer mixture and leave to marinate for 8–24 hours.
Cook the rack of ribs over a medium barbecue, turning occasionally, for 25–35 minutes until well browned and cooked through.
Yep! These really are flamin' tasty and no stickiness, y'all.

PERI PERI
pork and lemon

Peri peri chilli sauce is a Portugese condiment which is also popular in both Brazil and parts of Africa. It is sometimes known as piri piri or pili pili and is often served with chicken or fish, though I like it best with pork. Peri peri sauce is now available in most supermarkets.

SERVES 4
2 lemons
vegetable oil, for brushing
500g (1lb 2oz pork fillet
6 tablespoons peri peri sauce

TO SERVE
flat breads
salad

Very thinly slice the lemons and brush lightly with oil. Cut the pork fillet into rounds 1 cm ($^1/_2$ in) thick and brush with 1 tablespoon of the peri peri sauce.

Place a lemon slice on top of each piece of pork and pin in place with a cocktail stick. Cook over hot coals, lemon side down first, for 2–3 minutes on each side until well browned and cooked through.

Arrange on a serving platter with a little bowl of the remaining sauce for drizzling over. Have plenty of salad and flat bread to hand.

SMOULDERING
smoked Chinese roast ribs

Try this delicious marinade with any type of pork on the bone – the shoulder blade is particularly good. I like to serve these with the Stir-fried udon noodles (page 131)

SERVES 4
2 garlic cloves, crushed
1/2 teaspoon salt
4 tablespoons caster sugar
1 tablespoon hoisin sauce
1 tablespoon yellow bean sauce, Ainsley's barbecue
    sauce (page 22) or Oriental barbecue sauce (page 22)
2 tablespoons soy sauce
1 tablespoon Shaoxing rice wine or dry sherry
a few drops of red food colouring
1 sheet pork ribs (about 675 g/1 1/2 lb)

Mix together the garlic, salt, sugar, hoisin sauce, yellow bean sauce, soy sauce, rice wine and food colouring.
Place the ribs in a roasting tin and pour over the marinade. Refrigerate for an hour or so, basting occasionally with the mixture.
Cook the ribs over medium coals or under a pre-heated grill for about 40 minutes, turning occasionally and brushing over the remaining marinade, until cooked through. Carve between the ribs and serve.

Smouldering smoked Chinese roast ribs

PALENQUE PORK
and creambean tacos

I make this the traditional Mexican way by slow-barbecuing, or even slow-roasting it, and then slicing it into thin strips. This recipe is also a great way to use up cold pork left over from a roast.

SERVES 6
1 kg (2 1/4 lb) boned, rolled shoulder or leg of pork
salt and freshly ground black pepper
1 tablespoon vegetable oil
1 large onion, finely chopped
4 tomatoes, roughly chopped
2 dried smoky chillies, finely chopped, or a good pinch of chilli flakes
4 tablespoons chopped fresh coriander
1 x 400 g (14 oz) can kidney beans

TO SERVE
6 taco shells
bunch of salad onions, finely sliced
2 avocados, skinned, stoned and finely diced
lime wedges to garnish
sour cream (optional)

Season the pork with salt and pepper and cook in a covered barbecue over low-medium coals, or in an oven preheated to gas mark 4, 180°C (350°F), for 2 hours until well browned and cooked through.
Allow the pork to cool, then slice very thinly. Break the slices into long strips.
Heat the oil in a large pan and cook the onion for 3–4 minutes until beginning to soften.
Stir in the chopped tomatoes, chillies and coriander and cook for 5 minutes. Add the pork and season to taste.
Meanwhile, gently heat the beans in a small pan, then roughly mash.
Briefly warm the taco shells over hot coals or under a medium grill, then divide the mashed beans between them. Pile the pork mixture on top, sprinkle over the salad onions and avocado dice and serve each with a lime wedge for squeezing over.
A drizzle of sour cream can really add to the experience...

BARBECUED
sweet 'n' sour pork

Here I've taken a classic dish and cooked it all on the barbie. I think you'll like it – it certainly made a big impression with all my guests. You can always cook the pork in a frying pan if the British weather keeps you indoors.

SERVES 2

1 tablespoon dry sherry
300 g (10 oz) loin of pork, thinly sliced
salt and freshly ground black pepper
1 tablespoon cornflour
1 small egg, beaten
vegetable oil, for deep frying

FOR THE SAUCE

1 tablespoon vegetable oil
4 salad onions, thinly sliced
2 garlic cloves, thinly sliced
1 yellow pepper, diced
2 tablespoons wine vinegar
2 tablespoons tomato purée
1 tablespoon soy sauce
3 tablespoons clear honey
1 teaspoon sesame oil
100 ml (3 1/2 fl oz) water
boiled white rice to serve

Sprinkle the sherry over the pork and season well. Mix the cornflour with about half of the beaten egg and add to the pork a little at a time, tossing well to coat the meat.

Oil the barbecue bars or rack, then cook the pork for 2–3 minutes on each side until well browned.

Meanwhile, make the sauce: heat the vegetable oil in a large pan and cook the onions, garlic and pepper for 3–4 minutes until softened.

Stir in the vinegar, tomato purée, soy sauce, honey, sesame oil and water and bring to the boil. Add the barbecued pork and simmer for 4–5 minutes until cooked through. Serve with white rice.

CLARE'S CHINESE
crispy bubbled belly pork

Now here's one of my wife Clare's favourites. This is an easy way to make lovely, crispy Chinese-style pork, which looks dramatic and exciting on the barbecue. Go on, burst some bubbles. You won't be disappointed.

SERVES 6
approximately 1.5 litres (2 $\frac{1}{2}$ pints) boiling water
2 tablespoons salt
1.5 kg (3 lb) sheet belly pork
2 tablespoons soy sauce
2 teaspoons Chinese five-spice powder

FOR THE SAUCE
3 tablespoons soy sauce
3 tablespoons dry sherry
1 tablespoon dark brown sugar
a pinch of dried chilli flakes
2 cm ($\frac{3}{4}$ in) piece root ginger, finely chopped
white rice to serve

Pour a kettleful of boiling water over the skin of the pork and pat dry with kitchen paper. Rub the salt into the pork fat and leave to dry for 45 minutes.

Wipe the excess salt off the pork with kitchen paper, then, using a small, sharp knife, deeply score the pork skin in a criss-cross lattice. Turn the meat over and pierce the flesh in several places with a skewer. Rub the soy sauce and five-spice powder into the pork and set aside to marinate for an hour or so.

Cook over medium-hot coals, skin side down first, for 30 minutes on each side until cooked through with a very crunchy crackling.

Meanwhile, make the sauce: heat the soy, sherry, sugar, chilli and ginger together in a small pan, stirring until the sugar dissolves. Remove from the heat and allow to cool.

Slap the crispy bubbled pork on to a chopping board and cut the pork into 2 cm ($\frac{3}{4}$ in) wide slices. Transfer to a platter, and serve with rice and the dipping sauce.

Right: Claire's Chinese crispy bubbled belly pork with
Stir-fried udon noodles (page 131)
Below: Paddling through the creeks of the Rio Negre ricefields

HONEY FIRE-GLAZED
gammon with piled pineapple salsa

Treat yourself to a real feast and serve these sticky gammon steaks
with baked potatoes, a dollop of soured cream and Spicy lime-charred
corn on the cob (page 122).

SERVES 2
2 x 175 g (6 oz) smoked gammon steaks
5 cm (2 in) piece root ginger
1 tablespoon clear honey
1 teaspoon soy sauce
1 tablespoon vegetable oil

FOR THE SALSA
1 x 250 g (9 oz) fresh pineapple
1 tablespoon vegetable oil
juice of 1 orange
2 tablespoons light muscovado sugar
1 garlic clove, crushed
2 tablespoons wine vinegar
4 salad onions, finely chopped
2 red chillies, seeded and finely chopped
10 fresh basil leaves, shredded
salt and freshly ground black pepper

To make the salsa cut the top and bottom off the pineapple then slice
off the skin. Cut the pineapple into 8 even-sized wedges. Brush with
the oil and barbecue over hot coals for 3–4 minutes on each side until
golden and a little charred.

Mix together the orange juice, sugar, garlic, vinegar, salad onions and
chillies in a large bowl. Cut the pineapple wedges widthways into
chunks, stir into the mixture, then allow to cool a little.

Meanwhile, using a small pointed knife, make about 8 small slits in
each gammon steak. Peel the ginger and cut into 16 thin pieces. Push
a piece of ginger right into each slit so that it is visible on either side
of the steak.

Whisk together the honey, soy sauce and oil and brush over the
gammon. Cook over medium coals for 8–10 minutes on each side until
cooked through, shiny and a little charred around the edges.

Stir the basil into the salsa and season to taste. Arrange the gammon
steaks on a plate and pile on the salsa.

DIRTY RED'S
jump-up jambalaya

This is the most famous dish in Creole cookery. A jambalaya has absolutely no rules and you can throw in pretty well whatever you like – it's certainly worth singing about. The dish is getting on for 300 years old, the word 'jambalaya' being a combination of *jambon*, French for ham, and *ya*, which was old African slang for rice. Like our Storming Louisiana chicken and sausage gumbo (page 51), this recipe uses the trinity of green pepper, celery and onion.

SERVES 8
salt and freshly ground black pepper
6 spicy pork sausages, such as Lincolnshire or
    Cumberland
4 boneless pork loin chops
4 unskinned boneless chicken thighs
25 g (1 oz) butter
4 garlic cloves, finely chopped
2 small chillies, seeded and finely chopped
the trinity (see note with recipe for Storming Louisiana
    chicken and sausage gumbo, page 51)
4 tomatoes, roughly diced
1 tablespoon paprika
1 teaspoon dried thyme
1 litre (1 $^3/_4$ pints) chicken stock
500 g (1 lb 2 oz) long-grain rice
1 bunch of salad onions, finely chopped
4 tablespoons chopped fresh parsley

Season the sausages, pork chops and chicken and cook over medium coals for 10 minutes, turning once, until well browned.

Melt the butter in a large pan and cook the garlic, chillies and trinity for 3–4 minutes until beginning to soften. Stir in the tomatoes, paprika and thyme and cook for a further 3–4 minutes until the tomatoes are softened.

Cube the pork, chicken and sausage and add to the pan with the stock, rice, salad onions and half the parsley. Season generously and cook for 30 minutes or so, adding a little water if it becomes too dry, until the grains are tender. Spoon into bowls, sprinkle with the remaining parsley and serve.

EL PASO PORK
and prawn sticks

I've taken a uncomplicated recipe from a delightful restaurant in El Paso and created a great little dish. Yes, big juicy prawns and succulent pieces of spicy Spanish sausage – simple and delicious. I've used chorizo sausage but you could use smoked pork – the result is equally stunning.

SERVES 4
20 unshelled, raw tiger prawns
300 g (10 oz) chorizo sausage, cut into
   20 even-sized chunks
2 tablespoons olive oil
2 teaspoons balsamic vinegar
1 small garlic clove, crushed
10 fresh basil leaves, finely shredded
salt and freshly ground black pepper

TO SERVE
rocket
crusty bread

Thread the prawns and chorizo alternately on to 8 skewers. Cook over hot coals for 2–3 minutes, turning frequently, until the prawns are pink.
Meanwhile, whisk together the oil, vinegar, garlic and basil. Add salt and pepper to taste.
Pile the rocket on to 4 serving plates and place 2 skewers on each. Drizzle over the dressing and serve with crusty bread and lots of chilled Mexican beers.

Otto, the chef at O.T.s in Alabama, wants to know if it's true what they say about bald men. Yes, but only when I take my hat off!

PULLED PORK
sandwiches

In North Carolina, they smoke young hogs in dug-out pits over many hours to produce smoked meat that simply falls off the bone – it's known as pulled pork. I do my own version of pulled pork using a home smoker, and it works brilliantly. The secret is to start cooking the pork skin-side down and never to turn it. (See notes on home smoking with the recipe for Johnny Boy's hickory-smoked Cod, page 107, and on page 181.)

SERVES 6
salt and freshly ground pepper
1 x 2.75 kg (5 lb) shoulder of pork
1 small loaf of crusty bread, sliced, or 6 large, soft baps
Ainsley's barbecue sauce (page 22)

Prepare the smoker according to the manufacturer's instructions with a combination of charcoal and wood. Season the pork generously and cook in the smoker for 7–8 hours until completely cooked through.

Cut the meat off the bone, then, using two forks, shred the flesh into long strands.

Sandwich the pork in the bread or baps and top with a good dollop of barbecue sauce.

FIRE-FIST ALCAPULCO
chorizo quesadillas

These really are great and, if you get all organized before your guests arrive, they can do the final bit of cooking for themselves. The real beauty is that you end up holding these cones in your fist – hence the poetic name.

SERVES 4
1 teaspoon vegetable oil
1 small onion, finely chopped
2 garlic cloves, finely chopped
2 green chillies, seeded and cut into thin strips
100 g (4 oz) chorizo sausage, roughly chopped
225 g (8 oz) cooked potatoes, coarsely mashed
150 g (5 oz) Cheddar, or other tasty cheese grated
2 tablespoons chopped fresh coriander
salt and freshly ground black pepper
8 corn or flour tortillas

TO SERVE
sweet chilli sauce
soured cream

Heat the oil in a pan and cook the onion, garlic and chillies for 2–3 minutes until softened, Add the chorizo and cook for a further couple of minutes until the sausage is dark and crispy.
Add the potato, stirring until heated through. Remove from the heat, stir in the cheese and coriander and season to taste.
Heat two or three tortillas at a time on the barbecue or one at a time in a large, non-stick frying pan. Spread some of the potato mixture on top, then quickly fold into quarters. Cook for a minute or so on each side until crisp and golden brown, wrap in a paper napkin.
Ripple together a little soured cream and sweet chilli sauce and dollop a small spoonful on top of each quesadilla.

BEEF

LYNDA'S LAZY
lemon-rub steak with charred tomato salsa

One of my series' directors Lynda made me film this at least four times in Chicago because she adored the taste – I'm sure you will too.

SERVES 2
grated rind of 1 lemon
2 garlic cloves
1/2 teaspoon black peppercorns
1/2 teaspoon cumin seeds
1 teaspoon dried oregano
1/2 teaspoon cayenne pepper
1/2 teaspoon coarse sea salt
2 x 175 g (6 oz) sirloin steaks

FOR THE SALSA
3 plum tomatoes
a small bunch of fresh coriander
a small bunch of fresh mint
1 red onion, finely chopped
1 fresh green chilli, finely chopped
2 tablespoons olive oil
juice of 1/2 lemon
rock salt and freshly ground black pepper
leafy salad to serve

Using a pestle and mortar, a mini food processor or a coffee grinder, grind the lemon rind, garlic, peppercorns and cumin seeds together until well blended. Add the oregano, cayenne and salt and grind again.
Rub the mixture into the meat; set aside for an hour or two.
Meanwhile, halve the tomatoes lengthways and place on the barbecue, cut side down, for 5–8 minutes until softened and a little charred. Slip off the skins and roughly chop the flesh.
Finely chop the herbs and mix with the tomato, onion, chilli, olive oil and lemon juice; season well to taste.
Barbecue the steaks for 3–4 minutes on each side. Serve each with a good dollop of charred tomato salsa and a leafy green salad. Wow!

Lynda's lazy lemon-rub steak with charred tomato salsa

KOZAK'S
asado

Asado is the Argentinian word for barbecue and is particularly associated with Patagonia in the southern part of the country, where the legendary South American horsemen, the gauchos, cook their meat on open fires.

I like to serve my version of asado (named in honour of my producer Sara Kozak) with the Twice-baked hot-coal potatoes (page 126).

SERVES 6
1 x 1 kg (2 $1/4$ lb) fillet of beef
1 tablespoon olive oil
2 teaspoons dried rosemary

FOR THE HOT SAUCE
1 large onion, finely chopped
2 tomatoes, seeded and finely chopped
1 green pepper, seeded and finely chopped
2 hot red chillies, seeded and finely chopped
100 ml (3 $1/2$ fl oz) red wine vinegar
1—2 tablespoons caster sugar
2 tablespoons olive oil
salt and freshly ground black pepper

Begin by making the hot sauce. Stir together the onion, tomatoes, green pepper, chillies, vinegar, sugar to taste, olive oil and plenty of seasoning. Set aside at room temperature for at least an hour.
Thread 2 long metal skewers through the length of the meat and brush with the olive oil. Season generously and sprinkle with the rosemary. Cook the beef over medium coals, turning occasionally, for 30—60 minutes, according to how well done you like it.
Allow the meat to rest for a good 5 minutes, then carve and serve with the hot sauce.

REUBEN'S
favourite fajitas burritos

This is a cross between Mexican-style sizzling fajitas and tortilla burritos and it works a treat. If I'm making it for my kids, I sometimes throw a handful of grated cheese into each parcel so that they're scrumptiously melty and oozy when cut open.

SERVES 2

300 g (10 oz) sirloin steak
1 orange pepper, cut lengthways into 1 cm ($^1/_2$ in) wide strips
1 red onion, cut into 8 wedges
$^1/_2$ teaspoon dried oregano
$^1/_2$ teaspoon fennel seeds
1 tablespoon sunflower oil
4 x 20 cm (8 in) flour tortillas
1 x 150 ml (5 fl oz) carton soured cream or Cool, soft and smooth guacamole (page 134)
sunflower oil for brushing
salt and freshly ground black pepper
salad to serve

Cut the sirloin steak into strips 1 cm ($^1/_2$ in) wide. Place the pepper, onion, oregano, fennel seeds and sunflower oil in a bowl. Season generously and toss well together.

Cook the pepper strips and red onion on a sturdy baking sheet over the barbecue or in a large frying pan for 5 minutes, turning occasionally until they begin to soften and char. Add the steak strips to the barbecue and cook for 1–2 minutes on each side until browned. Remove the peppers, onions and steak from the barbecue and set aside.

Briefly warm 1 tortilla on the barbecue or in a non-stick frying pan for just a few seconds on each side until it is soft and will fold without cracking.

Spoon a quarter of the steak mixture on to the tortilla and top with a spoonful of soured cream or guacamole. Fold the edges over to enclose the filling and make a neat, square package. Skewer on either side with a cocktail stick to secure. Repeat with the other 3 tortillas.

Brush the parcels with a little of the sunflower oil and cook for 2–3 minutes on each side until crisp and golden brown. Serve hot with plenty of salad.

BOURBON BEEF
and blue cheese pancake wraps

This is a really quick dish once you start cooking – gather your friends round the barbecue and as soon as the steak is cooked, get them warming and rolling their own pancakes.

I cooked this on the roof of the Peabody Hotel in Memphis using Tennessee whiskey by the name of 'Dickel'. If you can't get a real Tennessee whiskey, don't worry – Bourbon will do.

SERVES 4
400 g (14 oz) 1 cm ($1/2$ in) wide strips of steak
3 tablespoons Tennessee whiskey or bourbon
$1/4$ teaspoon mustard powder
1 tablespoon vegetable oil
2 garlic cloves, thinly sliced
1 teaspoon Worcestershire sauce
salt and freshly ground black pepper
12 Chinese-style pancakes
150 g (5 oz) blue cheese, such as Roquefort
   or Gorgonzola
Tabasco to serve

Place the beef, whiskey and mustard in a non-metallic bowl and set aside to marinate for an hour or so.
Heat a sturdy baking sheet over hot coals, then drizzle over the oil. Cook the beef and garlic for 2 –3 minutes, stirring until well browned. Sprinkle over the Worcestershire sauce, then add a little salt and plenty of black pepper.
Briefly warm the pancakes over the coals, then crumble a little of the blue cheese over each. Add a few strips of beef, top with a shake of Tabasco and roll. Eat immediately.

QUICK–FIRED
steaks with anchovy-pepper dressing

Steak and anchovy sounds like an odd combination, but this tastes fantastic. I knocked this up in Buenos Aires using the most amazing Argentinian beef and it was a great hit. I love to serve it sandwiched between two slices of bread or, if I really feel like treating myself, I top it with a fried egg for a great breakfast.

SERVES 4
6 tablespoons olive oil
2 tablespoons red wine vinegar
6 anchovies in olive oil, finely chopped
$1/2$ teaspoon freshly ground black pepper
rock salt and freshly ground black pepper
12 x 50 g (2 oz) very thinly sliced fillet steaks
2 tablespoons finely chopped fresh parsley
green salad to serve

Place the oil, vinegar, anchovies and pepper in a small pan and simmer gently for 2–3 minutes on the side of the barbie.
Meanwhile, season and cook the steaks over very hot coals or in a pre-heated griddle pan for 30 seconds on each side, then transfer to serving plates.
Stir the parsley into the dressing and pour over the steaks. Serve with a green salad.

Japanese-style seared beef rolls (page 86)

JAPANESE-STYLE
seared beef rolls

Fans of Italian carpaccio will love this Japanese-inspired version of
very quickly seared meat. I've used daikon, which is a type of radish
also known as mooli – you can always use a regular radish and swap
the wasabi for a bit of creamed horseradish, if necessary.

SERVES 4
2 tablespoons soy sauce
1 tablespoon sake
1 teaspoon chilli oil
500 g (1 lb 2 oz) fillet beef

FOR THE SALAD
75 g (3 oz) rice noodles
1 tablespoon finely chopped pickled ginger
1 tablespoon toasted sesame seeds
3 tablespoons roughly chopped fresh coriander
4 salad onions, finely chopped
1 teaspoon sesame oil
1 tablespoon soy sauce

FOR THE DIPPING SAUCE
4 tablespoons soy sauce
1 tablespoon rice vinegar
1 tablespoon finely grated daikon
2 tablespoons water
wasabi to serve

Mix together the soy, sake and chilli oil and add the beef. Set aside at
room temperature for 30 minutes or so, turning from time to time.
To make the salad, place the noodles in a large bowl and cover with
boiling water. Set aside for a few minutes, then drain well and cool
under cold water. Mix with the ginger, sesame seeds, coriander, salad
onions, sesame oil and soy sauce.
Cook the beef over hot coals for 5 minutes, turning frequently until
the outside is well browned, then allow to rest for a couple of minutes.
For the dipping sauce, mix together the soy sauce, rice vinegar,
daikon and water. Divide between 4 small dipping bowls.
Slice the beef as thinly as possible and arrange on a serving platter.
Invite diners to smear a slice of beef with wasabi, place a little
noodle salad in the centre, then roll up and dip in the sauce.

BARBIE ARGIE
empanadas

Empanadas are spicy Argentinian patties traditionally served with chimichurri (page 16), but I prefer them with brown sauce. Ooh, Ainsley!

SERVES 6
500 g (1 lb 2 oz) plain flour
$1/4$ teaspoon salt
125 g ($4\,1/2$ oz) butter, melted
1 egg, beaten
200 ml (7 fl oz) warm water

FOR THE FILLING
1 tablespoon vegetable oil
350 g (12 oz) minced beef or chicken
4 salad onions, finely chopped
1 tablespoon paprika
$1/2$ teaspoon dried chilli flakes
2 tablespoons tomato purée
$1/4$ teaspoon ground cumin
50 g (2 oz) small seedless raisins
2 hard-boiled eggs, roughly chopped
50 g (2 oz) stoned green olives, roughly chopped
salt and freshly ground black pepper
vegetable oil for brushing

TO SERVE
Scrumptious snap carrot salad (page 135)
Chilled chickpea and yogurt salad (page 134)

To make the dough, sift the flour and salt into a large bowl. Stir in the butter and half the egg, then gradually work in enough warm water to make a firm dough. Knead vigorously for 5–10 minutes until the dough is smooth; cover it with a cloth and allow it to rest for 15–30 minutes.
For the filling, heat the oil in a large pan and cook the beef or chicken, salad onions and paprika for 4–5 minutes until well browned. Stir in the chilli flakes, tomato purée, cumin, raisins, hard-boiled eggs and olives. Simmer together for 5 minutes; season and leave to cool.
Roll out the dough to a thickness of about 3 mm ($1/8$ in). Cut round a saucer to make 24 circles 12 cm ($4\,3/4$ in) in diameter. Divide the filling between the dough circles and moisten the edges. Fold over to enclose the filling, then press down well to seal.
Brush the empanadas with a little oil and cook over medium coals for 4–5 minutes on each side until golden. Serve warm with the salads.

SAUSAGES & BURGERS

WILD BOAR
and cranberry patties with citrus cucumber

I cooked these delicious and really quite sophisticated burgers while travelling down the river in a *Voyageur* canoe in Quebec. It was the most beautiful setting and the fragrant, juicy burgers were set off perfectly with ribbons of lemony cucumber. I used wild boar because it's a popular meat there, but minced pork is a good substitute.

SERVES 4
100 g (4 oz) fresh or frozen cranberries, roughly
    chopped
500 g (1 lb 2 oz) finely minced wild boar or pork
6 salad onions, finely chopped
3 garlic cloves, crushed
2 teaspoons finely chopped fresh rosemary
grated rind and juice of 1 lemon
salt and freshly ground black pepper
1 cucumber
1 teaspoon salt

TO SERVE
1 loaf rustic bread
2 tablespoons olive oil

Mix together the cranberries, pork, salad onions, garlic, rosemary, lemon rind and plenty of seasoning.
Shape into 8 even-sized patties and cook for 5 minutes on each side until well browned and cooked through.
Thinly slice the cucumber lengthways into thin ribbons using a swivel-style vegetable peeler (discard the seedy part in the middle). Sprinkle over the salt, squeeze over the lemon juice and set aside for 5 minutes.
Cut the bread into 12 slices 1 cm ($1/2$ in) thick and brush with a little olive oil. Toast on each side, then lay a couple of strips of lemon cucumber on each slice. Place a patty on top of each and serve.

Wild boar and cranberry patties with citrus cucumber

SMOKING SAUSAGES
with night-owl vodka

I know that this is quite a time-consuming way to cook what is essentially a hot dog, but the fantastically tasty results are really worth the effort. I love to cook this on a weekend when I'm doing a bit of gardening, and here's my favourite part…once I've finished cooking, I pour some vodka into a strong glass jar and leave it in the smoker until it completely cools. Later on, once the smoker's cold, I lift out the vodka and I can tell you, it tastes amazing. (See notes on home smoking with the recipe for Johnny Boy's hickory-smoked cod, page 107, and on page 181.)

SERVES 4
8 large pork sausages
1 quantity of Orange marinade (page 10)
1 large onion, very thinly sliced into rings
1 teaspoon olive oil
salt and freshly ground black pepper
4 tablespoons wholegrain mustard

TO SERVE
crusty bread rolls
ketchup

Pierce the sausages in several places and place in a shallow dish. Pour over the marinade and set aside for at least a couple of hours.
Fire up the smoker with charcoal and your choice of wood (see page 181); I particularly like both mesquite and apple wood for this dish.
Toss the onion rings with the oil and little seasoning and place in a small roasting tin. Spoon the mustard into a heatproof dish.
If you have a double-layered smoker, drain the sausages, discarding the marinade, then place on the bottom rack and the mustard and onions on the top rack. Cover and smoke for 2–3 hours or so until the sausages are cooked through.
Split open the rolls and spoon in the onions. Place the sausages in the rolls and top with a spoonful of the smoky mustard and a squirt of ketchup.

SANTOS SAUSAGES
with Bavru banana mash

This recipe has a combination of flavours that work really well together, and is one I'm sure you'll enjoy. The idea came to me after visiting a restaurant in Bavru, just west of Santos, Brazil. Everything sounded like a mish-mash of flavours, but tasted great. I like to sandwich left-overs between two slices of bread and slap it back on the barbie for a scrumptious hot toastie.

SERVES 2
4 large ripe bananas
4 large pork sausages
1 tablespoon Dijon mustard
4 rashers dry-cure streaky bacon
25 g (1 oz) butter
2 tablespoons chopped fresh coriander
1 teaspoon cayenne pepper
salt and freshly ground black pepper

Cook the bananas in their skins over medium coals for 20 minutes until blackened and very soft.

Pierce the sausages in several places, then smear with the mustard. Stretch the bacon across the back of a knife and wrap round the sausages. Cook alongside the bananas for 20–25 minutes or so until the bacon is crispy and the sausages are cooked through.

Peel the bananas and place in a large bowl and mash until smooth. Mash in the butter, coriander and cayenne and add salt and pepper to taste.

Serve the sausages with a dollop of the Bavru banana mash on the side. Mmm, yummy!

MONZARELLI'S
Mediterranean burgers

This dish has all my favourite Mediterranean flavours in it: pine nuts, basil, sun-dried tomatoes, garlic and Parmesan – delicious.

SERVES 4
500 g (1 lb 2 oz) good-quality sausagemeat
8 sun-dried tomatoes in oil, very finely chopped
2 garlic cloves, finely chopped
2 tablespoons freshly grated Parmesan
2 tablespoons toasted pine nuts, roughly chopped
2 tablespoons shredded fresh basil
2 tablespoons chopped fresh parsley
salt and freshly ground black pepper

Place the sausagemeat in a large bowl and stir in the sun-dried tomatoes, garlic, Parmesan, pine nuts, basil, parsley and plenty of seasoning.

Using damp hands, shape the mixture into 4 even-sized burgers. Cook over medium coals for 5–6 minutes on each side until well browned and completely cooked through. Serve with nice Italian bread such as ciabatta, and hearty red wine.

Right: Monzarelli's Mediterranian burgers with Spicy lime-charred corn on the cob (page 122) and Crazy crunchy crispy coleslaw (page 132)

92

BRILLIANT BARBIE
butter bean burgers

Sometimes, I like to have a burger barbecue party, where I make a range of three or four different burgers and have a tableful of all the essential sauces, salads and accompaniments. They're always a great success and the bean burgers are a particularly big hit – and not just with the vegetarians.

SERVES 4
1 tablespoon vegetable oil, plus extra for brushing
1 onion, finely chopped
2 garlic cloves, finely chopped
1 red chilli, seeded and finely chopped
1 x 400 g (14 oz) can butter beans, drained and rinsed
50 g (2 oz) fresh white breadcrumbs
1 egg, beaten
juice of $\frac{1}{2}$ lemon
salt and freshly ground black pepper
2 tablespoons shredded fresh basil
75 g (3 oz) mozzarella, cut into 4 even-sized pieces

TO SERVE
salad
mayonnaise
burger buns

Heat the oil in a small pan and cook the onion, garlic and chilli for 4–5 minutes until softened and golden.
Meanwhile, mash the beans in a large bowl, then stir in the onion mixture, breadcrumbs, egg, lemon juice, basil and plenty of seasoning. Shape the mixture into 4 balls and push a piece of mozzarella into each burger. Gently flatten out the burgers, taking care to ensure the cheese is still completely enclosed.
Brush the burgers with a little oil and cook over medium coals or in a large non-stick frying pan for 3–4 minutes on each side until the burgers are golden and the cheese is oozy inside. Slap between buns and serve with mayo and salad.

THE GIANT KIDDY
beef burger

This is actually quite a classic burger, but I've made it more fun for kids by creating a giant one and serving it cut up into wedges.

SERVES 6
500 g (1 lb 2 oz) minced beef
1 sweet and sour pickled gherkin, finely chopped
2 garlic cloves, finely chopped
4 tablespoons chopped fresh parsley
salt and freshly ground black pepper

TO SERVE
ketchup
mustard
mixed salad
crusty bread

Place the mince, gherkin, garlic, parsley and a good measure of salt and pepper in a large bowl and mix together well.
Shape into a large round about 2 cm ($\frac{3}{4}$ in) thick. Transfer to a sturdy baking sheet and cook over hot coals or in a large frying pan for 5–10 minutes on each side until well browned but still a little pink in the centre.
Cut into wedges, squirt over a little ketchup and mustard and serve with plenty of salad and some crusty bread.

STUDDED LAMB
peppercorn patties

If you like that warm, peppery taste, this is for you. I've coated these juicy lamb burgers in crushed peppercorns, just like a peppered steak. They're crunchingly stunning...

SERVES 4
500 g (1 lb 2 oz) minced lamb
1 bunch salad onions, finely chopped
4 garlic cloves, finely chopped
1 tablespoon chilli sauce
$^1/_2$ teaspoon salt
1 tablespoon Dijon mustard
2 tablespoons coarsely crushed black peppercorns

TO SERVE
salad
Summery chilli chop salsa (page 15)
chips

Place the lamb, salad onions, garlic, chilli sauce and salt in a large bowl and mix together well. Shape the mixture into 4 even-sized burgers, then smear both sides with a little mustard.
Sprinkle with peppercorns, then cook over hot coals or under a pre-heated grill for 3–4 minutes on each side until crusted and golden on the outside but still a little pink in the centre. Serve with salad, my Summery chilli chop salsa and chips.

INSIDE-OUT
chicken chilli burgers

I don't like shop-bought chicken burgers as they have an unpleasant, synthetic flavour. It's so easy to make tasty ones yourself at home and they're even tastier cooked over coals. The chilli is not overpowering, as my kids will testify. 'Cor, Dad, these are wicked!'

SERVES 4
500 g (1 lb 2 oz) minced chicken
2 garlic cloves, crushed
1 red chilli, seeded and finely chopped
1 tablespoon chopped fresh mint
2 tablespoons chopped fresh parsley or coriander
2 teaspoons Worcestershire sauce
salt and freshly ground black pepper
olive oil, for brushing

TO SERVE
burger buns
salad
Garlic mayonnaise (page 99)

Mix together the chicken mince, garlic, chilli, herbs, Worcestershire sauce and plenty of salt and pepper.
Shape the mixture into 4 even-sized burgers, then brush lightly with the oil.
Cook on a medium barbecue for 5 minutes on each side until well browned and cooked through. Serve in burger buns with salad and Garlic mayonnaise.

SEAFOOD

SALMON BUTTER
pit-pocket knots

Sometimes a recipe can tickle your tastebuds even before you've prepared it... This one easily falls into that salivating category.

If you can't get long chives, tie shorter ones together.

SERVES 2
25 g (1 oz) butter at room temperature
2 garlic cloves, finely chopped
5 black olives, finely chopped
1 teaspoon sun-dried tomato paste
salt and freshly ground black pepper
2 x 150 g (5 oz) thick salmon fillets
6 large sage leaves
2 Parma ham slices
2–6 long chives
lemon wedges to serve

Mix together the butter, garlic, olives, sun-dried tomato paste and plenty of seasoning until well blended.

Cut a deep, 5 cm (2 in) long slash across the centre of each salmon fillet, taking care not to cut right through. Spread the butter mixture into the slit, then smooth the surface evenly.

Arrange the sage leaves over the slash, enclosing the butter. Place each salmon fillet sage side down in the centre of the ham and fold over the edges. Knot a chive round each parcel to secure.

Cook the salmon over hot coals for 4 minutes on each side until the Parma ham is crispy and the salmon is just cooked through. Serve with lemon wedges for squeezing over.

Salmon butter pit-pocket knots

CHARLES'
charred seafood rice

All those delightful flavours and aromas captured in one pot plus all the fun of cooking seafood over hot coals...you just can't beat it. My mate Charles is the king crab cracker, so this is one is named after him.

SERVES 6
2 red peppers

2–3 tablespoons olive oil

1 large onion, finely chopped

4 garlic cloves, finely chopped

450 g (1 lb) rice (you can use any rice
   you wish, apart from pudding rice!)

450 ml (15 fl oz) white wine

750 ml (1¼ pints) hot chicken stock

salt and freshly ground black pepper

1 large cooked lobster

6 large crab claws

2 limes, 1 squeezed and 1 cut into 6 wedges

500 g (1 lb 2 oz) live mussels (optional)

12 unshelled raw prawns

1 fresh red chilli, seeded and finely chopped

4 tablespoons chopped fresh parsley

Cook the whole red peppers close to the hot coals for 8–10 minutes, turning frequently until blackened and blistered.

Heat 2 tablespoons of the oil in a large pan placed on the barbecue rack. Add the onion and garlic and cook for 3–4 minutes until beginning to soften. Stir in the rice and cook for 1 minute, then add the wine and cook for 4–5 minutes, stirring occasionally until all the liquid has been absorbed.

Stir the hot stock and plenty of seasoning into the rice pan and cook the rice for a further 15 minutes until the grains are tender.

Meanwhile, skin and seed the pepper, cut the flesh into thins strips and stir into the rice pan.

Remove the claws from the lobster and crab and crack the claws with a hammer or heavy stone, leaving the shell on. Brush the claws with olive oil, sprinkle over a little lime juice and cook on the barbecue for 2–3 minutes on each side.

Using a cleaver, cut off and discard the lobster head. Leaving the shell on the lobster, cut the tail into pieces at each section and stir into the rice with the legs and mussels, if using; cook for a further 5 minutes until the mussel shells have opened (do not eat any unopened mussels).

Brush the prawns with a little oil, sprinkle over some lime juice, season well and sprinkle with fresh chilli. Cook for 1–2 minutes on each side until lightly charred.

Arrange the prawns on top of the seafood rice with the claws; sprinkle over the chopped parsley and serve garnished with lime wedges.

QUIDI VIDI
fishcakes with garlic mayonnaise

I cooked these fishcakes in the beautiful fishing harbour of Quidi Vidi, Newfoundland, and, boy, were they tasty!

SERVES 4

1 x 150 g (5 oz) piece salt cod, soaked in cold water for 24 hours
3–4 tablespoons olive oil
450 g (1 lb) cold boiled potatoes, roughly mashed
1/2 teaspoon ground cumin
large bunch of chives, snipped
1 egg, beaten
a few shakes of Tabasco
salt and freshly ground black pepper
1 teaspoon cumin seeds

FOR THE GARLIC MAYONNAISE

1 large egg yolk, at room temperature
a squeeze of lime or lemon juice
150 ml (5 fl oz) mixed sunflower and olive oil
4 garlic cloves, crushed
salt

Drain the salt cod, brush with a little olive oil and cook on a hot barbecue for 2–3 minutes on each side until soft enough to flake the flesh.

Meanwhile, make the garlic mayonnaise: place the egg in a large bowl with a squeeze of lime juice and whisk until well blended. Gradually beat in the oil to make a smooth, thick mayonnaise. Stir in the garlic and add salt to taste.

Pull the skin off the fish and discard. Flake the fish, discarding any bones, then stir into the mashed potato mixture with the ground cumin, all but 1 tablespoon of the chives, the beaten egg and Tabasco; season lightly.

Shape the mixture into 4 even-sized cakes. Brush lightly with olive oil and sprinkle with the cumin seeds.

Barbecue or fry for 2–3 minutes on each side until golden. Serve with a dollop of garlic mayonnaise and a sprinkling of the reserved chives.

SUCCULENT
sardines with minted tomato and orange salad

If you are using fresh vine leaves, remove the stems and cook the leaves in boiling, salted water for 4–5 minutes; cool under running water and they're ready to wrap.

SERVES 4
1 lemon, thinly sliced
1 lime, thinly sliced
1–2 tablespoons olive oil
12 preserved or fresh vine leaves (see recipe introduction)
12 x 75 g (3 oz) fresh sardines, cleaned
salt and freshly ground black pepper
crusty bread to serve

FOR THE SALAD
2 large oranges, peeled and sliced
2 large tomatoes, sliced
1 red onion, thinly sliced
2 tablespoons olive oil
juice of $1/2$ lemon
1 tablespoon chopped fresh mint, parsley or basil

Brush the lemon and lime slices with olive oil and cook over hot coals for 1–2 minutes on each side until lightly charred.

Place the vine leaves in a large bowl and cover with boiling water. Leave for a couple of minutes, then cool under cold running water.

Lay the vine leaves out flat and place a lemon or lime slice on each leaf. Sit a sardine on top and season generously. Place another citrus slice on each sardine, then drizzle over a touch of olive oil.

Wrap the leaves around the fish to make parcels and secure each with a short, soaked bamboo skewer or cocktail stick. Cook over hot coals for 3–4 minutes on each side until cooked through.

Meanwhile, arrange the oranges, tomatoes and red onion on 4 large serving plates. Whisk together the olive oil, lemon juice, herbs and a little seasoning.

Arrange the sardines on top of the salad bed and spoon over the dressing. Serve with crusty bread for mopping up all the lovely juices.

Succulent sardines with minted tomato and orange salad

ALAN AND ANDY'S
Amazonian fish kebabs

I used a freshwater Amazonian fish for the programme, but you'll get the best results from monkfish. I've combined the fish here with some English and Oriental flavourings and made some pretty tasty skewers. Always use a good-quality chilli oil that contains shrimp paste so that you get flavour as well as heat.

I've named these kebabs after Alan, my cameraman, and Andy, my soundman – they're a real double act.

SERVES 4
500 g (1 lb 2 oz) cubed monkfish
2 tablespoons soy sauce
1 tablespoon tomato purée
juice of 1 lime
1 tablespoon vinegar
1 tablespoon clear honey
$1/2$ teaspoon fish sauce
$1/2$ teaspoon chilli oil
1 tablespoon fresh chopped coriander
Stir-fried udon noodles (page 131) to serve

Thread the monkfish on to 8 skewers.
Mix together the soy sauce, tomato purée, lime juice, vinegar, honey, fish sauce, chilli oil and coriander, then brush over the kebabs.
Cook the skewers over hot coals or under a pre-heated grill for about 6–8 minutes, turning frequently, until the fish is cooked through and a little charred. Serve on a bed of stir-fried noodles.

FIREPAN COCONUT
mussels

I love to serve these with freshly cooked chips or even some barbecued potato wedges for dipping in the yummy coconut sauce. I use my old roasting tin for this, but you can use any large, sturdy pan.

SERVES 2
1 tablespoon sunflower oil
1 teaspoon Thai green curry paste
1 garlic clove, finely chopped
1 tablespoon finely chopped root ginger
$^1/_2$ teaspoon ground turmeric
1 x 150 ml (5 fl oz) carton coconut cream
2 kaffir lime leaves, shredded (optional)
1 lemon grass stalk, finely chopped
1 kg (2$^1/_4$ lb) fresh mussels
2 teaspoons fish sauce
1 teaspoon caster sugar
juice of 1 lime
a handful of fresh basil leaves, roughly torn

Place a roasting tin directly on to hot coals or on the stove top and add the oil. Cook the curry paste, garlic and ginger for 1–2 minutes. Add the turmeric, coconut cream, lime leaves and lemon grass and bring to the boil.

Add the mussels and cook for 7 minutes or so, shaking the pan occasionally, until the mussel shells open (discard any that remain closed).

Sprinkle over the fish sauce, caster sugar and lime juice and stir well to distribute. Remove from the heat and transfer to serving bowls. Scatter over the basil leaves and serve hot.

Overleaf: And you thought your neighbour's house was bright! (St John's, Newfoundland)

CHARLES PART'S
river eel with potacado salad

Canadian chef Charles cooked us a dish using local river eel which
was delicious. Mackerel and salmon make good alternatives to the eel.

SERVES 4
1 x 550 g (1 ^{1}/$_4$ lb) skinless river eel or 4 x 150g (5 oz)
  boneless, unskinned mackerel or salmon fillets

FOR THE MARINADE
3 tablespoons soy sauce
3 tablespoons sake
2 tablespoons rice vinegar
2 tablespoons caster sugar
1 teaspoon finely chopped pickled ginger
1 garlic clove, crushed
1 tablespoon sunflower oil
^{1}/$_2$ teaspoon sesame oil
1 tablespoon roughly chopped fresh coriander

FOR THE SALAD
500 g (1 lb 2 oz) baby new potatoes, cooked and diced
2 ripe avocados, skinned, stoned and diced
1 large red onion, diced
juice of 2 limes
4 tablespoons olive oil
2 tablespoons toasted sesame seeds
4 tablespoons fresh coriander leaves
salt and freshly ground black pepper

Begin by making the marinade: place the soy sauce, sake, rice
vinegar, sugar, ginger, garlic, sunflower and sesame oils in a small
pan. Slowly bring to the boil, stirring until the sugar dissolves, then
simmer for 5 minutes. Allow to cool, then stir in the coriander, pour
over the fish and set aside to marinate for a couple of hours.
Meanwhile, prepare the salad: toss together the diced potatoes,
avocados, red onion, lime juice, olive oil, three-quarters of the sesame
seeds and 3 tablespoons of the coriander leaves. Season generously
and chill until ready to serve.
Cook the fish over hot coals or in a non-stick frying pan for 3–4
minutes on each side (depending on the thickness), basting with the
marinade until just cooked through.
Pile the salad on to a serving plate and place the fish on top. Garnish
with the remaining coriander and sesame seeds.

JOHNNY BOY'S
hickory-smoked cod with a soft cheese dressing

Most home smokers are American-made and each individual model needs to be operated according to its specific instructions, so I am going to keep my recommendations very flexible and ask you to check your manual before you start to cook.

I have a double-layered smoker, so often choose to cook a few separate dishes or ingredients at the same time and serve them together, as in this recipe. The smoke penetrates the oil-based dressing, which is then is cut cleanly through with the creaminess of the soft cheese.

Remember – never open the smoker during the process or you will have to add about 15 minutes to your cooking time. If you need to check on your food or fuel, do so only by the access door.

SERVES 4
2 garlic cloves, finely chopped
1 hard-boiled egg, roughly chopped
4 tablespoons olive oil
salt and freshly ground black pepper
4 x 150 g (5 oz) cod fillets or other white fish fillets
2 tablespoons chopped fresh parsley
100 g (4 oz) soft cheese
1 tablespoon lemon juice

TO SERVE
salad
crusty bread

First heat up your smoker with a combination of charcoal and hickory chips.
Place the garlic, egg, olive oil and a little salt and pepper in a heatproof bowl.
Arrange the fish over the bottom rack. Place the bowl of dressing on the top rack and smoke for 1 hour or so until the fish flakes easily.
Gradually beat the dressing and parsley into the soft cheese (you might need to do some vigorous whisking with a fork to blend it together) and add salt, pepper and a squeeze of lemon juice to taste.
Arrange the fish on serving plates and spoon over a dollop of the dressing. Serve with salad and crusty bread.

CRUSTED CHILLI
sprat fish fans

Good supermarkets now stock sprats and, of course, your local fishmonger will always get them for you if they're not in stock already.

SERVES 4
16 sprats, cleaned
salt and freshly ground black pepper
lemon or lime wedges to serve

FOR THE FILLING
2 tablespoons chopped fresh parsley
2 garlic cloves, crushed
grated rind of 1 lime

FOR THE COATING
4 tablespoons plain flour
2 teaspoons cayenne pepper
2 tablespoons olive oil

Make the filling by mixing together the parsley, garlic and lemon rind.
Open each fish and season the cavity and sprinkle in a little of the parsley mixture.
Place 4 fish in a row then angle them so that the tails are on top of each other with the fish splayed out like a fan. Tie a piece of string around the tails to hold the fish in position. Repeat to make 4 fish fans.
Place the flour, cayenne and some salt and pepper in a large shallow dish. Brush the fish fans with olive oil, then dust them with the seasoned flour. Cook over hot coals or in a large frying pan for 3–4 minutes on each side until golden brown and cooked through.

What an entrancing sight – the 'hunchback' mountain of Rio de Janeiro emerging through the mist after an afternoon rainstorm

HEAVENLY
herb-tied tuna

I've used a selection of my favourite fragrant herbs with tuna for this recipe, but you can vary the herbs and fish that you use. Other good combinations using this method include salmon with sage or cod with rosemary and strips of lemon peel.

SERVES 4
4 x 200 g (7 oz) tuna steaks
2 tablespoons olive oil, plus extra for serving
salt and freshly ground black pepper
8 rosemary sprigs
8 thyme sprigs
8 bay leaves

TO SERVE
salad leaves
1 lemon, quartered

Brush each tuna steak with oil and season generously with salt and pepper. Tie a piece of string around the tuna in both directions, as if making a parcel.

Slip a rosemary sprig, thyme sprig and bay leaf under the strings of each steak, then turn over and do the same on the other side. You can cover the fish and chill for several hours at this stage, if you wish.

Cook over hot coals or in a griddle pan for 2–3 minutes on each side until the tuna is nicely coloured and just cooked through. Place each tuna steak on a bed of salad leaves, drizzle with some olive oil and serve with a lemon quarter for squeezing over.

ORIENTAL BARBECUED
cod tent corners

I use extra-strong foil to make a tent in which the cod can steam in its own juices – it gives a very delicate, fragrant result. The real beauty of this dish is the delightful aroma that fills the air and your nostrils when you pop open the tent corner.

SERVES 4
4 x 150 g (5 oz) cod fillets
1 x 10 cm (4 in) piece root ginger, cut into matchsticks
6 salad onions, shredded
2 garlic cloves, finely chopped
2 tablespoons soy sauce
1 tablespoon wine vinegar
1 teaspoon sesame oil
noodles or rice to serve

Arrange the cod fillets in the centre of 4 large squares of foil. Scatter over the ginger, salad onions and garlic. Drizzle each piece of fish with a little soy sauce, vinegar and sesame oil. Pull 2 corners of the foil together and fold over the edges to make a tent around each fish.
Barbecue over medium coals for 8 minutes until the fish is just cooked. Serve with noodles or rice.

VEGETARIAN

OOZING ORIENTAL
stuffed aubergine slices

It looks good, it tastes great and it's ideal for that special barbecue date. Get all Oriental – get stuffing.

SERVES 4
2 large aubergines
sunflower oil for brushing
salt and freshly ground black pepper
50 g (2 oz) glass noodles, or other thin rice noodles
1 large carrot, cut into matchsticks
50 g (2 oz) bean sprouts
2 cm ($^3/_4$ in) piece root ginger, finely chopped
a handful of fresh coriander leaves
1 tablespoon toasted sesame seeds
1 tablespoon hoisin sauce
1 tablespoon soy sauce

TO SERVE
boiled rice and soy sauce
Garlic herb-tucked and tossed tomatoes (page 123)

Diagonally cut the aubergine into 16 oval slices, 1 cm ($^1/_2$ in) large.
Brush the aubergine slices with oil on one side only, season and place on the barbecue rack for 4–5 minutes over medium-hot coals until golden brown.
Meanwhile, place the noodles in a bowl and cover with boiling water. Set aside for 2–3 minutes, or according to packet instructions, then drain.
Mix together the carrot, bean sprouts, ginger, coriander leaves, sesame seeds, hoisin sauce, soy sauce and drained noodles.
Place 8 slices of the aubergine, cooked side uppermost, on a flat surface and spoon the noodle mixture into the centre of each. Top with the remaining aubergine slices, ensuring that the uncooked surface is on the outside.
Using soaked 12 cm (4 $^3/_4$ in) bamboo skewers pin each aubergine sandwich closed along the long edges, to enclose the filling. Brush with a little more oil and cook for 2–3 minutes on each side until the aubergine is cooked and golden.

Oozing Oriental stuffed aubergine slices

CHARRED COUSCOUS
pepper cups

You can buy couscous everywhere now. It's a craze which has gripped the nation and I, for one, am not surprised – it goes with anything, especially my tasty pepper cups.

SERVES 2
2 large red peppers
75 g (3 oz) couscous
150 ml (5 fl oz) hot vegetable stock
2 yellow or orange tomatoes, finely diced
4 tablespoons chopped fresh parsley
4 sun-dried tomatoes in oil, finely chopped
50 g (2 oz) blue cheese, crumbled or diced
2 tablespoons olive oil
salt and freshly ground black pepper

Halve the peppers lengthways, keeping the stalks intact. Remove the core and seeds, then cook over medium coals, cut side down, for 5–8 minutes.
Place the couscous in a heatproof bowl and pour over the hot stock. Stir in the chopped tomatoes, parsley, sun-dried tomatoes, cheese and olive oil; season to taste.
Turn the peppers over and spoon the couscous mixture into them. Return to the barbecue and cook for 20–30 minutes until the peppers are softened and the bases are a little charred.

FIRE-TOASTED
tofu satay

I use smoked tofu for this as it has a much firmer texture than the usual variety and the flavour works very well on a barbecue.

SERVES 2
1 x 300 g (11 oz) pack smoked tofu
2 tablespoons soy sauce
1 tablespoon chilli sauce
1 tablespoon vegetable oil

FOR THE SATAY SAUCE
1 x 150 g (5 oz) carton coconut cream
4 tablespoons crunchy peanut butter
1 tablespoon soy sauce
juice of 1 lime

Cut the tofu into 2 cm ($3/4$ in) cubes. Stir together the soy sauce, chilli sauce and vegetable oil. Add the tofu cubes and set aside to marinate for 1–2 hours.
Place the coconut cream, peanut butter and soy sauce in a small pan and heat gently on the edge of the barbecue.
Thread the tofu on to skewers and barbecue over hot coals or in a griddle pan for a minute or so on each side until beginning to brown and crispen a little.
Squeeze the lime juice into the satay sauce, then serve drizzled over the smoked charred tofu skewers.

WARM HALLOUMI
pitta finger salad

Halloumi is a delicious Greek cheese that softens but doesn't melt, so it's great for barbecues – but make sure you eat it quickly because it turns slightly rubbery when cold.

SERVES 4
2 x 200 g (7 oz) halloumi, cut into slices 1 cm
  ($^1/_2$ in) thick

olive oil, for brushing
4 mini pittas, cut into triangular fingers
1 cos lettuce, roughly shredded
150 g (5 oz) baby plum tomatoes, halved lengthways
50 g (2 oz) kalamata olives

FOR THE DRESSING
1 tablespoon pickled capers, rinsed and
  roughly chopped
grated rind and juice of 1 lime
3 tablespoons olive oil
salt and freshly ground black pepper

Begin by making the dressing: stir together the capers, lime rind and juice, olive oil, a little salt and plenty of black pepper.
Brush the cheese with a little olive oil and cook over hot coals for 2 minutes on each side until golden. Heat the pitta fingers in the same way for about 30 seconds on each side.
Arrange the lettuce, tomatoes and olives on 4 serving plates. Place the pitta fingers and the cheese on top of the salad and drizzle over the dressing; eat warm.

SMOKED AUBERGINE
tomato and basil cannellini pasta

A large bowl of this served at any of my barbie parties never hangs around for long. It is simply bursting with lovely flavours.

SERVES 4
8 plum tomatoes, quartered
1 aubergine, cut into slices 1 cm ($^1/_2$ in) thick
4–6 tablespoons olive oil
salt and freshly ground black pepper
pinch of saffron strands
4 garlic cloves, halved
300 g (10 oz) lasagnette or tagliatelle
1 x 400 g (14 oz) can cannellini beans,
  rinsed and drained
handful of fresh basil leaves, roughly torn
freshly grated Parmesan to serve

Brush the tomatoes and aubergine slices with a little oil and season well. Cook the aubergines for 3–4 minutes on each side until softened and golden, and cook the tomato quarters for 2 minutes on each side.
Meanwhile, add the saffron and garlic to a large pan of boiling, salted water and cook the pasta according to the packet instructions.
Cut the cooked aubergine slices into strips 2 cm ($^3/_4$ in) wide and place in a large bowl with the tomatoes and cannellini beans.
Drain the pasta well and add to the bowl with the remaining olive oil and basil. Toss together well, check the seasoning and serve topped with grated Parmesan.

SPEEDY CORNZALES
cheesy parcels

I made these delicious parcels in the main square, the *Zócalo*, in
Oaxaca surrounded by locals and the local police! There was the small
problem of needing a filming permit, which had been sent to the wrong
address. So yours truly was incredibly speedy before we cheesed
off the Bill!

For this recipe I use dried corn husks and canned sweetcorn, but you
can always buy whole corn on the cob, save the husks and cook the
corn yourself.

SERVES 4

5 dried corn husks
1 x 400g (14 oz) can cannellini beans, rinsed
   and drained
200 g (7 oz) sweetcorn
4 tablespoons mayonnaise
1 bunch of salad onions, finely chopped
2 garlic cloves, finely chopped
4 tablespoons chopped fresh parsley
salt and freshly ground black pepper
a few drops of Tabasco
150 g (5 oz) Cheddar, grated, or mozzarella, roughly diced
salad to serve

Soak the corn husks in hot water for 15 minutes until soft and pliable.
Meanwhile, mash the cannellini beans and mix with the sweetcorn,
mayonnaise, salad onions, garlic and parsley. Add salt, pepper and
Tabasco to taste.
Open out 4 of the husks and divide half of the bean mixture between
them. Scatter over the cheese, then top with the remaining bean
mixture. Fold the edges in to enclose the filling and form a neat,
square parcel. Tear the remaining husk into strips 5mm ($1/4$ in) wide
and tie these around the centre of each parcel to hold it securely.
Barbecue over medium coals or under a pre-heated grill for
5–7 minutes on each side until the parcels are warmed through and
the husks well browned. Serve with lots of crunchy green salad.

Speedy cornzales cheesy parcels

AVOCADO CONE
quesadillas

When making quesadillas, the tortillas are usually stacked and then cut into wedges, but I prefer to fold them into little cones and serve them individually.

SERVES 4

8 corn or flour tortillas
150 g (5 oz) grated cheese, such as Monterey Jack,
   Cheddar or Wensleydale
lime wedges to garnish

FOR THE FILLING
2 tomatoes, seeded and diced
1 large avocado, skinned, stoned and diced
1 red onion, finely chopped
juice of $^1/_2$ lemon
a few drops of Tabasco
salt and freshly ground black pepper

FOR THE TOPPING
1 x 150 ml (5 fl oz) carton soured cream
2 tablespoons chopped fresh coriander

Make the filling: stir together the tomatoes, avocado and red onion, then stir in the lemon juice, Tabasco and season to taste.
Prepare the topping: mix together the soured cream and coriander, then season.
Assemble the quesadillas 2 or 3 at a time. Briefly heat the tortillas for a few seconds on each side, then sprinkle over some cheese followed by the avocado mixture. Quickly fold the tortillas in half and then in half again to make triangular shapes – you need to be speedy to prevent the tortillas crisping up too much before you fold them.
Cook for a further minute or so on each side until the tortillas are crisp and golden brown and the cheese has melted; repeat to make 8 quesadillas.
Arrange on plates and top each serving with a dollop of the soured cream mixture. Garnish with a lime wedge and serve warm.

ARTICHOKES
Niçoise

Step aside Mr Green Bean, here comes the artichoke kid and he makes the best Niçoise in town.

SERVES 4
4 large globe artichokes
juice of 1 lemon
3 tablespoons olive oil
2 onions, sliced
4 garlic cloves, thinly sliced
2 thyme sprigs
4 tomatoes, seeded and diced
1 teaspoon caster sugar
100 ml (3$^1/_2$ fl oz) white wine
75 g (3 oz) fresh white breadcrumbs
50 g (2 oz) pitted black olives, roughly chopped
4 tablespoons chopped fresh parsley
salt and freshly ground black pepper

Slice the stalks off the artichokes so they sit flat. Pull off all the leaves until you get to the hairy choke in the centre. Carefully pull out the choke to leave just the heart of the artichoke. Add the lemon juice to a pan of boiling salted water and cook the artichoke hearts for 7–8 minutes until just tender; drain well.

Meanwhile, heat 2 tablespoons of olive oil in a large pan and gently cook the onion, garlic and thyme for 5–10 minutes until softened and golden. Add the tomatoes and sugar, cook for a couple of minutes, then pour in the wine, bring to the boil and cook rapidly for 2–3 minutes until the liquid evaporates.

Heat the remaining tablespoon of olive oil in a separate pan and cook the breadcrumbs for 2–3 minutes, stirring frequently, until crisp and golden brown.

Remove the onion pan from the heat and stir in the olives, parsley and half the breadcrumbs. Season the mixture to taste, then pile into the artichoke hearts and sprinkle over the remaining crumbs.

Brush the outside of the artichokes with a little oil and cook over medium coals or in a medium pan for 15–20 minutes, until tender and piping hot.

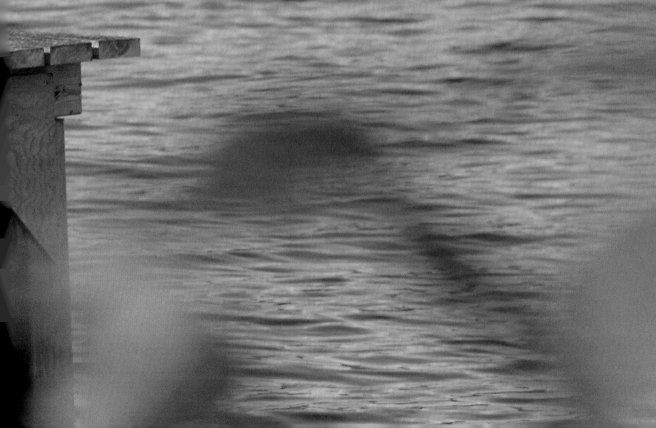

VEGETABLES, SIDE DISHES & BREADS

BARBECUE VEGETABLES

CHARRED TASTY
tatties

You can roast new potatoes from raw on your barbecue but they take a while to cook through. So why not pre-boil them for speediness and wonderful results, especially with this simple recipe.

SERVES 4
1 tablespoon grainy mustard
1 tablespoon clear honey
1 tablespoon soy sauce
400 g (14 oz) new potatoes, boiled

Mix together the mustard, honey and soy sauce. Halve the potatoes lengthways and toss in the mustard mixture. Thread on to skewers and cook for 2–3 minutes on each side until crisp and golden brown.

SPICY LIME-CHARRED
corn on the cob

There really is nothing like freshly barbecued corn on the cob. Some people like to peel off the husks, but I think they act as natural protection and prevent the kernels from becoming dry and hard.

SERVES 4
4 corn cobs
2 limes, each cut into 4 wedges
1 teaspoon salt
$1/4$ teaspoon cayenne pepper

Pull the husks back from the corn, then remove and discard the silks. Rub each corn cob with a wedge of lime, then fold back the husks to cover the kernels.
Cook over medium coals for about 10 minutes, turning frequently, until the corn is dark golden and the kernels tender.
Mix together the salt and cayenne pepper.
Pull the husks back away from the corn and sprinkle over the salt mixture. Serve with a wedge of lime for extra rubbing.

Previous page: Forget bottoms up. This is bottoms down with a glass or two of chilled wine and some great Canadian scenery.

CHOMPING
caponata

This Italian dish is best enjoyed warm or at room temperature, so if you are making it in advance and storing it in the fridge, remember to take it out a couple of hours before serving.

SERVES 6
2 aubergines, cut into 2 cm ($^3/_4$ in) cubes
1 red pepper, seeded and cut into 2 cm ($^3/_4$ in) pieces
1 yellow pepper, seeded and cut into 2 cm ($^3/_4$ in) pieces
6 ripe tomatoes, quartered
1 garlic bulb, halved widthways
6 tablespoons olive oil
sea salt and freshly ground black pepper
1 tablespoon balsamic vinegar
2 tablespoons dark muscovado sugar
150 g (5 oz) pitted black or green olives
2 tablespoons chopped mixed fresh herbs, such as parsley, coriander and chives to serve

Place the aubergines, peppers, tomatoes and garlic in a large roasting tin. Drizzle over 2 tablespoons of olive oil, season generously and mix well. Roast over medium coals or in a medium oven for around an hour, stirring from time to time, until the vegetables are softened and lightly charred.
To make the dressing mix together the remaining 4 tablespoons of olive oil, the vinegar and sugar, stirring until the sugar dissolves; season.
Stir the dressing and olives into the caponata and sprinkle over the herbs; serve warm or at room temperature, perhaps with a lovely bottle of nicely chilled Frascati?

GARLIC HERB-
tucked and tossed tomatoes

To capture all the wonderful flavours of this dish you simply must eat these tomatoes hot or, at least, warm.

SERVES 4–6
500 g (1 lb) pomodorino or cherry tomatoes
4 large garlic cloves
2–3 tablespoons olive oil
salt and freshly ground black pepper
3 red chillies, seeded and finely chopped
2 tablespoons chopped fresh parsley, chives or basil
juice of $^1/_2$ lemon

Arrange the tomatoes in a shallow roasting tin. Lightly flatten each unpeeled garlic clove with a heavy knife and tuck these and the chillies between the tomatoes.
Drizzle over the oil, season with salt and pepper and cook over hot coals for 15–20 minutes, stirring occasionally, until the tomatoes have softened.
Stir in the herbs and add lemon juice, salt and pepper to taste.

BUBBLING PESTO
mushroom cups

I love to make this with large-capped field mushrooms, but you can do it with smaller ones – you just need to make sure that they don't tip and spill the pesto juices.

SERVES 4

4 field mushrooms
olive oil for brushing
salt and freshly ground black pepper

FOR THE PESTO

2 tablespoons pine nuts
2 garlic cloves, roughly chopped
15 g ($^1/_2$ oz) fresh basil leaves
25 g (1 oz) butter
2 tablespoons freshly grated Parmesan
3 tablespoons olive oil

Brush the mushrooms with olive oil and season lightly. Cook gill-side down over medium coals or in a griddle pan for 5 minutes.

Meanwhile, place the pine nuts, garlic and basil in a food processor and whizz until very finely chopped. Add the butter and Parmesan and whizz again; then, with the motor running, slowly pour in the olive oil to make a thick paste. Season with a little salt and plenty of black pepper.

Turn the mushrooms over and divide the pesto mixture between them. Continue to cook for 10 minutes until the mushrooms are very tender and the pesto is bubbling.

**Right: Bubbling pesto
mushroom cups
Left: On the boards
in Newfoundland,
Canada**

TWICE-BAKED
hot-coal potatoes

Baking potatoes on a barbecue from raw takes a long time. I find this method means I can bake or microwave my potatoes, then re-crisp them on the barbecue. The longer you cook them, the crunchier the skin will be.

SERVES 4
4 x 200 g (7 oz) baked potatoes
1 tablespoon olive oil
$1/2$ teaspoon salt, plus extra to serve
butter to serve

Rub the potatoes with the oil, then sprinkle with salt. Cook over medium coals for 10–30 minutes, turning fairly frequently, until the skin is dark and crunchy.
Split open the potatoes, sprinkle over a little salt, drop in a nice knob of butter and serve piping hot.

DOUBLE DIP
spicy chips

To get good, crispy chips with a fluffy centre you need to cook them twice.

SERVES 4
4 large floury potatoes, such as King Edward or
  Maris Piper
vegetable oil for deep frying
cubes of bread for testing oil temperature
1–2 tablespoons Cajun or Creole seasoning
$1/2$ teaspoon salt

Peel the potatoes and cut into long, thin chips, then wash them thoroughly in cold water. Dry well with kitchen paper.
Pre-heat a deep-fat fryer. Test the temperature with a cube of bread until it turns golden in about 60 seconds: if the fat is too hot at this stage, the fries will turn brown before they are cooked. When the oil is ready, cook the chips for 3–4 minutes until pale golden.
Drain the fries on kitchen paper. Raise the oil temperature until a cube of bread browns in 30 seconds. Return the fries to the pan and cook for a minute or two until crisp and dark golden. Drain on kitchen paper, then sprinkle with the spicy seasoning and salt. Serve immediately.

FIERY CHILLI
broccoli sticks

I think broccoli tastes delicious when it's a little charred and still crunchy. These sticks are quite Italian, so I like to serve them with Aromatic charred bruschetta (page 136), a little bowl of olive oil and balsamic vinegar for dipping into, a bowl of strong black olives and maybe a few cubes of blue cheese. What a great light lunch!

SERVES 4
4 mild red chillies
1 small head of broccoli, cut into florets
1 tablespoon olive oil
sea salt

Cut the chillies into 2.5 cm (1 in) lengths (don't seed them) and place in a large bowl with the broccoli florets. Drizzle over the oil, sprinkle over the salt, then toss together well.
Thread the vegetables on to skewers and cook over very hot coals for 2–3 minutes until lightly charred in places. Serve immediately.

CHEESE AND BUBBLE
squeaky hotcakes

Perfect for those occasional leftover tatties. I vary the ingredients every time and they always taste great. Add whatever you have to hand: try adding pieces of cooked sausage, bacon or chorizo for a more substantial serving.

Make sure you use floury potatoes, such as King Edward or Maris Piper, as new potatoes aren't starchy enough to hold the cakes together. I cook them on a fine rack. If your barbecue has a wide-barred rack, use an oiled baking sheet instead.

SERVES 4
350 g (12 oz) boiled or baked potatoes
150 g (5 oz) cooked cabbage, Brussels sprouts,
   broccoli or spinach, shredded or chopped
1 garlic clove, finely chopped
50 g (2 oz) Cheddar, grated
a few shakes of Tabasco
salt and freshly ground black pepper
olive oil for brushing

Place the potatoes in a large bowl and mash thoroughly. Stir in the cabbage, garlic, cheese, a good dash of Tabasco and plenty of salt and pepper.
Shape the mixture into 4 even-sized cakes. Brush with a little oil and cook over medium coals or in a large frying pan for 4–5 minutes on each side until golden.

ROSEMARIED SWEET
potato parcels

Rosemary and sweet potato really do complement each other beautifully. Go on, you won't be disappointed.

SERVES 2
large knob of butter
4 sprigs of rosemary
2 x 425 g (15 oz) sweet potatoes
salt and freshly ground black pepper

Lightly butter four large squares or circles of foil and place a rosemary sprig in the centre of each.
Dice the sweet potatoes and divide between the squares. Season generously, then dot with a little more butter. Fold over the foil to enclose the sweet potatoes, then scrunch the edges together to seal.
Cook on a rack set over medium coals for 20–30 minutes, shaking the parcels occasionally until the sweet potatoes are tender, and a little charred.

**Right: Rosemaried
sweet potato parcels**

SALADS & SIDE DISHES

SAFFRON-SCENTED
rice

This is a really great side dish. I serve it both hot and cold and it really does go with just about all barbecued meat, chicken and fish.

SERVES 4
2 tablespoons olive oil
1 onion, finely chopped
2 garlic cloves, finely chopped
225 g (8 oz) long-grain rice
750 ml (1¹/₄ pints) hot vegetable stock
a pinch of saffron strands
a pinch of dried chilli flakes
2 tablespoons chopped fresh parsley or coriander
juice of ¹/₂ lemon

Heat the oil in a large pan and cook the onion and garlic for 5 minutes until softened and golden. Stir in the rice and cook for a minute or two, turning to coat the grains in oil.

Stir in the stock, saffron and chilli flakes. Bring to the boil and simmer for 20 minutes or so, until the grains are tender.

Stir in the parsley and lemon juice and serve.

RANCH-STYLE
pit baked beans

I served these here beans when I was down on the Benjamin Ranch in Kansas. Them cowboys sure did find 'em mighty fine!

SERVES 8
250 g (9 oz) dried white beans, such as navy or cannellini beans, soaked overnight
1 onion, finely chopped
100 g (4 oz) chorizo sausage or smoked bacon/ham, roughly chopped
3 tablespoons dark muscovado sugar
1 tablespoon soy sauce
1 teaspoon Worcestershire sauce
1 tablespoon English mustard

Place the beans in a large pan of fresh water, bring to the boil and boil hard for 10 minutes. Drain the beans and return to the pan.

Stir in the chopped onion, meat, sugar, soy and Worcestershire sauces and English mustard. Cover with water, then sit the pan directly on the coals.

Cook for 4–5 hours, stirring occasionally, until the beans are soft and tender. Serve with grilled pork sausages or ribs.

NOW, NOW!
refried beans

Real refried beans are a thick, porridgy paste that makes a great spoonable side dish or can be spread on to tortillas, stirred into spicy chillies or mixed with a little tomato juice for a yummy dip. If you prefer the chunkier, but less authentic version, just don't mash 'em too much.

Use whatever cheese you have to hand, but my absolute favourite for this dish is crumbly, creamy Wensleydale.

SERVES 4
2 tablespoons olive oil
1 small onion, finely chopped
2 garlic cloves, finely chopped
1 x 400 g (14 oz) can borlotti or kidney beans, drained and rinsed
salt and freshly ground black pepper
50 g (2 oz) cheese, crumbled or grated

Heat the oil in a large frying pan and cook the onion and garlic for 5 minutes until golden. Add the beans to the pan and cook for about 10 minutes, stirring and mashing the beans with a wooden spoon as you go.
If you find the mixture keeps sticking to the pan, add a little water, but try to avoid doing so, if possible. Season the mixture to taste, then stir in the cheese. Immediately remove from the heat and spoon into a serving bowl – you don't have to wait for the cheese to melt. Just get stuck in.
Serve hot as a side dish or allow to cool and use as desired.

STIR-FRIED
udon noodles

Udon are thick, white Japanese-style noodles but you can use any type of noodle you like for this dish – try regular Chinese-style egg noodles or the fine rice noodles. Mirin is a sweet sake used for cooking – you can use a medium sherry if you can't get hold of it.

I love to serve this with any Oriental-style food, including both Thai and Chinese. Try it as an accompaniment to Jim's fire-glazed duck with fresh plum dipping sauce (page 56), or Clare's Chinese crispy bubbled belly pork (page 72).

SERVES 6
250 g (9 oz) dried udon noodles
1 tablespoon vegetable oil
1 teaspoon sesame oil
3 cm (1$^{1}/_{2}$ in) piece of root ginger, finely chopped
2 garlic cloves, finely chopped
1 red chilli, seeded and thinly sliced lengthways
bunch of salad onions, shredded
4 tablespoons toasted sesame seeds (page 6)
2 tablespoons soy sauce
1 tablespoon mirin
a few drops of rice vinegar

Cook the noodles in a large pan of boiling water according to the packet instructions. Cool by rinsing under cold water, then drain well.
Heat the oils in a wok and stir-fry the cooked noodles, ginger, garlic and chilli for 3–4 minutes until just beginning to brown. Stir in the salad onions and sesame seeds and stir-fry for 1 minute.
Stir in the soy sauce, mirin and a few drops of rice vinegar, to taste. Turn into a large bowl and serve immediately.

CRAZY CRUNCHY
crispy coleslaw

I go for a mayo-free coleslaw. It's particularly good with barbecued chicken burgers and potato dishes.

SERVES 6
$1/2$ teaspoon cumin seeds
1 small white cabbage, shredded
1 small red onion, thinly sliced
2 tart green apples, cored and thinly sliced
2 red jalapeño chillies
3 tablespoons olive oil
1 teaspoon walnut oil (optional)
juice of 1 lime
1 teaspoon white wine vinegar
salt and freshly ground black pepper

Place the cumin seeds in a small non-stick frying pan and cook over a medium heat for a couple of minutes, until they begin to offer up a delightful aroma and turn a little darker.
Place the cabbage, onion, apples, chillies, oils, lime juice, vinegar and cumin seeds in a large bowl and toss together well. Season to taste and chill until needed.

SYD'S CHICORY,
blue cheese and walnut salad

This is a very stylish side salad. I once ate a starter in a restaurant in Sydney, Australia, that was very similar to this, only each chicory leaf was topped with a small, seared scallop. Why not serve this as an accompaniment to my Succulent seared scallops (page 32).

SERVES 4
50 g (2 oz) walnut halves
2 small heads of chicory
100 g (4 oz) blue cheese, such as Roquefort or dolcelatte, roughly crumbled into 1 cm ($1/2$ in) pieces
2 tablespoons olive oil
juice of $1/2$ lemon
salt and freshly ground black pepper

Roughly chop the walnuts, then toast in a non-stick frying pan for 2–3 minutes until golden brown; allow to cool.
Separate the chicory leaves and arrange on a serving platter. Scatter over the blue cheese and walnuts.
Whisk together the olive oil, lemon juice and a little salt and pepper. Drizzle the dressing over the salad and serve immediately.

Right: Syd's chicory, blue cheese and walnut salad

CHILLED CHICKPEA
and yogurt salad

Simple salads that are healthy and light, yet packed with flavour, are a favourite of mine. This one definitely falls into that category.

SERVES 6
1 tablespoon olive oil
$1/4$ teaspoon coriander seeds
$1/4$ teaspoon black mustard seeds
1 onion, finely chopped
2 garlic cloves, finely chopped
2 x 400 g cans chick peas, drained and rinsed
1 x 200 g (7 oz) carton Greek yogurt
2 tablespoons chopped fresh coriander
salt and freshly ground black pepper
juice of $1/2$ lime

Heat the oil in a small pan and cook the coriander and mustard seeds, onion and garlic for 3–4 minutes until golden brown.
Place the chick peas in a large bowl and stir in the onion mixture, yogurt and fresh coriander. Add salt, pepper and lime juice to taste. Chill until ready to serve.

COOL, SOFT
and smooth guacamole

This is such a versatile dish. It's great served with tortilla chips or crunchy vegetables as a snack or starter, or served with spicy fajitas, burritos or chillies to cool them down. However you choose to serve it, I'd never even think about putting together a Mexican meal without a little bowlful of guacamole on the side.

Avoid lumpy guacamole by choosing only nicely ripe avocados. The addition of water may seem a little unusual, but it loosens and softens the texture in a most delicious manner.

SERVES 2
1 garlic clove
1 green chilli
2 tablespoons chopped fresh coriander
1 large, ripe avocado
4–5 tablespoons water
juice of 1 lime
salt and freshly ground black pepper

Place the garlic, chilli and coriander in a food processor and whizz until finely chopped. Add the avocado flesh and whizz until completely smooth.
Gradually stir in the water until the mixture is very soft and smooth. Add lime juice, salt and pepper to taste. Chill until ready to serve.

SCRUMPTIOUS SNAP
carrot salad

I shred my carrots using a mandoline, as it makes brilliant long matchsticks, or my food processor, which has a nifty blade that does a similar job. If you don't have either, you can always grate the carrots, but they won't be as crisp or as snappy.

SERVES 4
500 g (1 lb 2 oz) carrots, shredded
1 garlic clove, crushed
$1/4$ teaspoon salt
a pinch of cayenne pepper
1 tablespoon red wine vinegar
2 tablespoons olive oil
2 tablespoons chopped fresh coriander
25 g (1 oz) salted peanuts, roughly chopped

Pile the carrots into a large serving bowl. In a separate bowl, whisk together the crushed garlic, salt, cayenne, vinegar and olive oil.

Pour the dressing over the carrots, add the coriander and peanuts and toss together well. For maximum snap, serve within an hour.

FLAMED
polenta chips

These little golden flamed nuggets have a lovely texture and go brilliantly with really full-on salsas and dips. See pages 15, 16 and 23 for recipes.

SERVES 6
1.2 litres (2 pints) boiling water
$1/2$ teaspoon salt
200 g (7 oz) instant polenta
25 g (1 oz) butter
olive oil for brushing

Place the water and salt in a large pan and return to the boil. Pour in the polenta, stirring constantly until smooth and thickened. Beat in the butter.

Pour the polenta on to an oiled baking sheet and spread out to a thickness of about 1 cm ($1/2$ in). Allow to cool completely.

Brush the top surface of the polenta with a little more oil, then cut into fingers 1 cm ($1/2$ in) wide.

Cook over medium coals for 3–4 minutes, turning until crisp and golden brown. Serve immediately with a salsa for dipping.

BARBECUE BREADS

AROMATIC
charred bruschetta

Bruschetta is simply Italian toast, but there are many ways of making it and it's often served with a selection of toppings. I'm keeping it really simple here – just make sure you give it enough time over the coals so that it catches and chars a little.

SERVES 4
1 small loaf of rustic bread
2 tablespoons olive oil
sea salt
2–4 garlic cloves

Cut the bread into slices 2 cm ($3/4$ in) thick and brush with the olive oil. Sprinkle with salt and cook over hot coals for a couple of minutes on each side until lightly toasted and a little charred in places.
Halve the garlic cloves and rub the cut surface over the bruschetta. The aroma is wonderful. Pile into a basket or arrange on a platter and serve warm.

Aromatic charred bruschetta with Wicked kicking salsa (page 16)

CHEESE
and Charleston cornbread

Although these are made in the oven, they are a welcome accompaniment to any barbecue party. Hot cornbread is automatically placed on the table of every restaurant in the southern USA. It's rich and crumbly, easy to make and tastes great – just like in Charleston, South Carolina.

SERVES 4
200 g (7 oz) yellow cornmeal
75 g (3 oz) plain flour, sifted
2 teaspoons baking powder
1 teaspoon salt
2 teaspoons caster sugar
1 onion, grated
1 tablespoon olive oil
1 egg, beaten
350 ml (12 fl oz) milk
1 tablespoon freshly grated Parmesan

Pre-heat the oven to gas mark 7, 220°C (425°F). Mix together the cornmeal, flour, baking powder, salt, caster sugar and onion. In a large jug, beat together the oil, egg and milk, then stir into the cornmeal mixture to make a smooth batter.

Pour into a 15 cm (6 in) square tin, sprinkle over the Parmesan and cook for 20 minutes until set and golden brown. Cut into wedges, slices or whatever you prefer... I like mine spread with chilled unsalted butter.

CHESTER'S
corn cakes

These are one of my dad Chester's favourites. Serve these tasty little cakes with sweet toppings, such as soft berries and Greek yogurt, for breakfast, or with strips of pulled pork (page 78) or Blackened chicken Chichen-Itzá (page 52) for a light lunch.

MAKES 12–18 CAKES
200 g (7 oz) cornflour
1 1/2 teaspoons baking powder
1/2 teaspoon salt
150 ml (5 fl oz) milk
1 tablespoon honey
25 g (1 oz) butter
2 eggs, separated
250 g (9 oz) corn kernels, thawed if frozen
oil for greasing

Sift the cornflour, baking powder and salt into a large bowl.

Pour the milk into a small pan and add the honey and butter. Heat gently until the butter melts, then remove from the heat; do not boil. Whisk the egg yolks into the liquid, then pour into the flour mixture, stirring to make a smooth batter. Stir in the corn kernels.

In a separate bowl, whisk the egg whites until they form soft peaks, then gently fold into the batter.

Brush a little oil on to a sturdy baking sheet or strong griddle set over medium coals. Spoon small rounds of the mixture on to the griddle and cook for 2 minutes on each side until golden.

SLAP HAND
Brazilian cheese buns

The expression 'slap hand' comes from my late mother who, every Sunday, would make slap hand rotis for lunch. I've taken the idea a little further.

MAKES 20 ROLLS
300 ml (10 fl oz) milk
25 g (1 oz) butter
450 g (1 lb) strong white bread flour, plus extra
   for dusting
1 teaspoon salt
$1/2$ teaspoon easy-blend dried yeast
50 g (2 oz) freshly grated Parmesan
1 large egg, beaten

Gently heat the milk and butter in a small pan. Once the butter has melted, the milk has reached the right temperature.
Sift the flour into a large bowl and add the salt, yeast and Parmesan. Stir in the warm milk and then the beaten egg to make a sticky dough. Cover the bowl with a tea towel and set aside for an hour or so in a warm place until the dough has doubled in size.
Dust a sturdy baking sheet with flour and place on a rack several inches above the barbecue coals. With floury hands, slap and shape the dough into small buns. Place them on the baking sheet and cook for about 5–8 minutes until browned and risen. Flip and cook for a further 5 minutes until cooked through. Serve hot from the barbecue.

TABLE-TOP
naan

The classic accompaniment to any saucy curry. Try it with my Alabama chicken Brummie balti on page 48.

MAKES 2 LARGE NAAN
250 g (8 oz) self-raising flour
1 teaspoon easy-blend yeast
1 teaspoon salt
3 tablespoons live natural yogurt
knob of butter

Place the flour, yeast and salt together in a large bowl and make a well in the centre. Add the yogurt and 5–6 tablespoons of warm water to make soft, slightly sticky dough.
Knead the dough on a floured surface for a minute or two then cover with a clean tea towel and leave in a warm place for around an hour until doubled in size.
Cut the dough in half and roll each piece out into a large rectangle. Cook over hot coals or under a pre-heated grill for about a minute on each side until puffed and lightly browned.
Smear each naan with butter and serve warm.

ELLEN'S CHICAGO
deli pizza

I cooked this while I was in Chicago, the home of American pizza and of my friend Ellen. The pizza stone I used was bought from a local cookshop and it gave a really good, crispy base. These stones are not expensive and I definitely recommend them – just make sure that the one you buy can withstand high temperatures, as some types may crack under the intense heat of the barbecue.

MAKES 2 LARGE PIZZAS
450 g (1 lb) strong white bread flour, plus extra
  for dusting
1 teaspoon easy-blend dried yeast
1 teaspoon salt
2 tablespoons chopped fresh parsley
2–3 tablespoons olive oil
300 ml (10 fl oz) warm water
selection of toppings, such as chorizo sausage, marinated
  vegetables, smoked cheese, olives and capers

FOR THE SAUCE
6 fresh tomatoes, roughly chopped
2 garlic cloves
$1/2$ teaspoon dried oregano
2 tablespoons olive oil
2 tablespoons tomato ketchup
salt and freshly ground black pepper

Sift the flour into a bowl and add the yeast and salt. Make a well in the centre and add the parsley, oil and warm water to make a soft dough. Knead the dough for 10 minutes until smooth and elastic. Rub a little oil into the surface of the dough, cover with plastic wrap and leave in a warm place for an hour or so until doubled in size.

Set a pizza stone or sturdy baking sheet directly on the warm coals and leave to heat up for 15 minutes. Dust generously with flour.

Meanwhile, make the sauce: place the tomatoes, garlic, oregano, oil and ketchup in a small pan and heat gently for 10–15 minutes until thickened and pulpy; season to taste.

Roll the dough into 2 circles 30 cm (12 in) in diameter and place on the stone or baking sheet.

Spoon the fresh tomato sauce over the dough and arrange your choice of toppings on the pizzas. Cook for 20 minutes until the dough is crisp and cooked through.

Ellen's Chicago deli pizza

WICKED BARBIE
smelted sarnies

Much tastier than a toastie, far more fantastic than French toast – the barbie sarnie is the best snack you could ask for. I love to serve it with a dollop of Wicked kicking salsa (page 16) or Chilli jam (page 19).

SERVES 2
4 slices white bread
1 tablespoon Dijon mustard
75 g (3 oz) Cheddar or other tasty cheese, grated
2 slices honey-roast ham
2 eggs, beaten
4 tablespoons milk
a few shakes of Tabasco
salt and freshly ground black pepper
4 tablespoons cornmeal
oil for brushing

Spread the bread with the mustard, place the cheese and ham on top, then put the slices together to make 2 sandwiches.
Beat together the eggs, milk, Tabasco and a little seasoning until well blended. Pour the mixture into a shallow dish large enough to take the sandwiches side by side. Leave to soak for several minutes, turning occasionally until all the liquid is absorbed. Sprinkle the sandwiches with the cornmeal until evenly coated.
Oil the barbecue bars and cook the sandwiches over medium coals for 3–4 minutes on each side until golden brown and smelted inside. Ooh, gorgeous!

BAKED GARLIC
and fennel flatbread

This is a really simple bread to make using pizza dough mix. It's also quite similar to the fancy foccacia breads you can pay a fortune for, so have a go. I'm sure you'll enjoy it.

MAKES 1 ROUND 25 CM (10 IN) LOAF
2 tablespoons olive oil, plus extra for drizzling
2 garlic cloves, finely chopped
145g pack pizza-base mix
125 ml (4 fl oz) warm water
2 teaspoons fennel seeds
sea salt

Pre-heat the oven to gas mark 7, 220°C (425°F). Heat the oil in a small pan, add the garlic and heat very gently for 5 minutes until the garlic softens but does not colour.

Empty the pizza-base mix into a large bowl. Make a well in the centre and add the water, garlic-oil mixture and fennel seeds. Mix gently to make a soft dough, then knead for 5 minutes until smooth.

Roll the dough to make a 25 cm (10 in) circle, transfer to a baking sheet and leave to rise for 20 minutes. Using your thumb, make indents all over the dough. Sprinkle over some sea salt and bake for 20 minutes until well risen and browned.

Drizzle some olive oil over the bread, then wrap it in a clean tea towel and set aside for 5–10 minutes or until completely cool – this is so that steam gathers beneath the tea towel and prevents the surface of the bread from becoming too crusty or hard. Eat warm.

DESSERTS
& DRINKS

BARBECUE DESSERTS

WINDY CITY
honey-grilled fruit with ember-roast almonds

We ate this juicy fruit dessert on the shores of Lake Michigan one sunny evening as the sun was beginning to set on the Chicago skyline. When I want to conjure up the memories, I get in my back garden, fire up my trusty old barbecue and, in less than 10 minutes, this is ready to serve and I'm back in the Windy City.

SERVES 4
100 g (4 oz) whole almonds
25 g (1 oz) butter
25 g (1 oz) caster sugar
2 peaches or nectarines, stoned and cut into wedges
12 whole strawberries
2 tablespoons clear honey
1 x 200 g (7 oz) carton crème fraîche
1 vanilla pod or a few drops of vanilla extract

Place the nuts on a double layer of foil and dot over the butter and sugar. Fold the foil over to enclose the nuts and cook them directly on the coals for 5–8 minutes, until the butter and sugar have melted to coat the nuts in a toffee mixture. Remove from the barbecue and allow to cool and set.

Thread the fruit on to 4 soaked bamboo skewers. Brush with the honey and cook over the hot coals for 1–2 minutes on each side until lightly charred.

Halve the vanilla pod and stir the seeds into the crème fraîche. Drizzle the vanilla crème fraîche on to the serving plate and arrange the skewers on top. Sprinkle over the toffee nuts and serve warm.

SOFT MERINGUES
with sweet avocado cream

In Brazil and Mexico, they often use avocado as a pudding ingredient – it has a very mild flavour and lovely creamy texture which blends well with milk and sugar, as in this splendid dessert. The avocados you use must be perfectly ripe or they will not mash smoothly.

SERVES 4
600 ml (1 pint) milk
a few drops of vanilla extract
3 egg whites
150 g (5 oz) caster sugar, plus 2 tablespoons
2 ripe avocados
juice of $1/2$ lime
prepared fruit, such as dried mango, banana and passion fruit to serve

Pour the milk and vanilla extract into a strong roasting tin and heat over medium coals without boiling.

Whisk the egg whites until very stiff, then add 150 g (5 oz) sugar and whisk again until smooth and shiny. Drop big spoonfuls of the meringue into the warm milk and cook for about 5–8 minutes, turning once, until set.

Meanwhile, halve, skin and stone the avocados, then mash until smooth. Stir in the remaining caster sugar.

Transfer the meringues to large plates.

Gradually beat about a quarter of the milk into the avocado to make a soft, smooth purée; add a little lime juice to taste. Divide the meringues between 4 serving bowls and spoon over a dollop of avocado cream. Top with the fruit and serve while warm.

Previous page: Trainspotting in Birmingham (Alabama) and not an anorack in sight.

K.S.C. FILO
refuellers with toffee mud sauce

This is a dish I prepared at the Kennedy Space Centre in Florida just hours before the launch of the Space Shuttle Discovery, which hurtled John Glenn back into space after 36 years! I was even kitted out in a real astronaut suit.

SERVES 4
4 sheets filo pastry
25 g (1 oz) butter, melted
100 g (4 oz) soft cheese
100 g (4 oz) chopped strawberries or small raspberries
2 tablespoons icing sugar, sifted
vanilla ice cream to serve (optional)

FOR THE SAUCE
150 ml (5 fl oz) milk
100 g (4 oz) milk chocolate
50 g (2 oz) cream toffees

Place a sheet of pastry on the work surface, brush with a little butter and top with a second sheet of pastry. Sandwich together the other 2 sheets of filo with a little butter in the same way.

Cut each pastry 'sandwich' lengthways into 4 strips roughly 10 cm (4 in) wide. Place a dollop of soft cheese at the top of each filo sheet, scatter over some fruit and a sprinkling of icing sugar, then fold down the pastry to enclose the filling and make neat triangular parcels.

Brush each parcel with a little butter and cook over medium coals for 4–5 minutes on each side until the pastry is crisp and golden brown.

Meanwhile, pour the milk into a pan and break in the chocolate. Stir in the toffees and heat gently, stirring, to make a smooth, thick sauce.

Arrange the strawberry cheesecake pastries on serving plates and drizzle over the chocolate sauce. Top them with a dollop of vanilla ice cream.

SWEET CINNAMON
bread

Sweet fried bread is a popular street snack in South America – my version has a touch of the Spanish about it with the addition of sherry. Make sure you eat it as soon as it's out of the pan.

SERVES 4
4 slices of day-old fruit bread or white bread
100 ml (3 $^1/_2$ fl oz) sweet sherry
2 eggs
grated rind of 1 lemon
light olive oil, for shallow frying
caster sugar and ground cinnamon, for dusting
crème fraîche or single cream to serve

Cut the crusts off the bread and cut each slice diagonally in half to give triangles. Place the bread in a large shallow dish and drizzle over the sherry.

Whisk the eggs and lemon rind together in a separate shallow dish.

Heat a little oil in a large, heavy-based frying pan. Dip the sherry-soaked bread in the beaten egg mixture, then shallow fry on each side until the bread is puffy and golden brown.

Dust with caster sugar and cinnamon and serve warm with a dollop of créme fraîche or a drizzle of cream.

HONEYPONE
blueberry shortcakes

I love these old-fashioned-style shortcakes and was so pleased when I got them to cook nicely on the barbecue. I've used blueberries, but you can use any soft berries, such as strawberries or raspberries. Go on Honeypone, get cooking...

SERVES 8
400 g (14 oz) self-raising flour
1/2 teaspoon salt
100 g (4 oz) caster sugar
125 g (4 1/2 oz) butter
2 eggs
5 tablespoons milk

FOR THE FILLING
1 x 250 g (9 oz) carton mascarpone cheese
2 tablespoons clear honey
250 g (9 oz) blueberries
icing sugar for dusting

Sift the flour into a large bowl and add the salt and sugar. Rub in the butter until the mixture resembles breadcrumbs. Make a well in the centre. Beat together the eggs and milk and pour into the well; bring together to make a very soft dough.

Place a griddle or sturdy baking sheet on the barbecue over medium-hot coals or on the stove top and dust lightly with flour. If it burns instantly, it's too hot.

Shape the dough into 8 even rounds and cook them four at a time, spaced well apart on the griddle because they will spread as they rise. Cook for 8 minutes on each side until risen and golden brown. Transfer to a wire rack to cool.

Meanwhile, make the filling: mix together the mascarpone and honey until well blended. Split open the shortcakes horizontally and spread the honey mascarpone over the bottom half. Scatter over the blueberries and replace the lid. Dust with icing sugar and serve.

Right: Honeypone blueberry shortcakes
Below: Well you've gotta have a laugh, haven't you?

OAXACA CHOCOLATA
omeletta

The beautiful Mexican town of Oaxaca (pronounced Wahaca) is 5000
feet above sea level and this is where you can buy the rich cocoa
powder grown on the coast. The taste is wonderful... But you don't
need to use Oaxaca cocoa – simply buy a tin at your local supermarket
or swap the cocoa and caster sugar for $1\,^1/_2$ tablespoons of drinking
chocolate.

SERVES 1
2 eggs, separated
2 teaspoons cocoa powder, sifted
1 tablespoon caster sugar
a small knob of butter
2 tablespoons crème fraîche
icing sugar for dusting

Mix together the egg yolks, cocoa powder and caster sugar. In a
separate bowl, whisk the egg whites until they form soft peaks, then
gently fold them into the chocolate mixture.

Melt the butter in a small skillet set over medium-hot coals. Pour in
the egg mixture and cook for 2 minutes until the underneath is set.
Very carefully flip the omelette with a palette knife and cook the
second side for a minute or two.

Heat a metal skewer directly on the coals. Drop the crème fraîche on
top of the omelette, then flip it in half. Slide on to a plate and dust
heavily with sugar. Quickly press the hot skewer on to the sugar-dusted
omelette several times so that it caramelizes the sugar to leave criss-
cross branding marks. Serve immediately.

MAPLE FIRE
fruitbread pudding

You ideally need a kettle-style barbecue to cook this pudding, and if you have any wood chips to hand, throw them over the coals to make a bit of sweet smoke.

SERVES 4
300 g (11 oz) fruit bread, such as panettone,
  thinly sliced
butter for greasing, plus an extra knob
50 g (2 oz) whole almonds, roughly chopped
1 x 300 ml (10 fl oz) carton double cream
4 tablespoons maple syrup
vanilla ice cream to serve

Arrange the fruit bread slices, overlapping, in a buttered roasting tin, scattering the nuts as you go.
Place the cream, syrup and a knob of butter in a small pan and heat gently, stirring until the butter melts. Pour the cream mixture over the fruit bread, then cook over medium coals for 15–20 minutes, until bubbling and crusty around the edges.
Spoon the pudding into bowls and add a scoop of vanilla ice cream. Serve warm. Delicious!

DO-AHEAD DESSERTS

PAPOS BRAZILIAN
babas

These are a very popular dessert in Brazil, where they are called *papos de anjo*, which translates as 'angel's chins'. They remind me of little rum babas.

MAKES 12
3 large egg yolks
100 g (4 oz) caster sugar
200 ml (7 fl oz) water
1 vanilla pod
grated rind of 1 small orange

TO SERVE
crème fraîche
cinnamon for dusting

Pre-heat the oven to gas mark 6, 200°C (400°F). Whisk the egg yolks with an electric beater for about 8–10 minutes until pale and thickened. Spoon the mixture into a 12-hole buttered mini-muffin tin and cook for 15–20 minutes until golden and set.

Meanwhile, place the sugar in a pan with the water and bring slowly to the boil, stirring until the sugar dissolves. While the mixture is heating, split open the vanilla pod, scrape out the seeds and add to the pan with the orange rind. Once the sugar has dissolved, bring the syrup to the boil and simmer rapidly for a minute or two. Pour the syrup into a large heatproof bowl.

Remove the 'chins' from the oven and slip out of the tins. Drop into the syrup and leave to cool. Refrigerate for a few hours or overnight, remove the vanilla pods, then serve with a dollop of crème fraîche and a dusting of cinnamon.

Papos Brazilian babas

BRAZILIAN COCONUT
and coffee rice pudding

They're really big on coconuts in Brazil, and as I love nothing better than a good old rice pudding, I thought I'd mix the two together with a little of the local coffee for a truly scrumptious dessert. I like to serve it warm but cold is equally delicious and, if you time it right, it will be ready after you've tucked into one of my tasty main barbecue dishes.

SERVES 4
300 ml (10 fl oz) milk
1 x 400 ml (14 fl oz) can coconut milk
100 g (4 oz) pudding rice
50 g (2 oz) caster sugar
3 tablespoons strong black coffee

Place both milks, the rice, sugar and coffee in a large saucepan on the edge of the barbie and slowly bring to the boil. Simmer gently for 30–40 minutes, stirring, until the rice is tender. Serve warm, or allow to cool, then chill until ready to serve.

MERIDA ORANGE
sunset caramels

These scrumptious puds are similar to crème caramels. Instead of milk, I've used fresh orange juice and the end result reminds me of a beautiful Mexican Merida sunset. To die for.

SERVES 4
100 g (4 oz caster), sugar plus 1 tablespoon
4 tablespoons water
1 whole egg
2 egg yolks
300 ml (10 fl oz) fresh orange juice

Pre-heat the oven to gas mark 4, 180°C (350°F). Place the sugar and water in a small pan and heat gently, stirring, until the sugar dissolves. Bring to the boil and cook rapidly without stirring until the mixture turns dark amber.
Pour the caramel into 4 ramekins, swirling so it covers the base and sides; set aside to cool and harden.
Place the egg, egg yolks, orange juice and 1 tablespoon of caster sugar in a large bowl and whisk until well blended and frothy. Pour into the ramekins and place these in a roasting tin. Pour water into the tin so that it comes two-thirds up the side of the ramekins. Bake for 30–40 minutes until set.
Allow the puddings to cool, then chill for 8–24 hours. Turn out on to small serving plates and serve.

KHARM KEY
lime pie

Alright so the correct word is charm, but don't the title look nice?

This pie is traditionally cooked with a meringue topping. I keep mine simple and serve it with cream – don't worry if it cracks in the oven, that's part of its kharm.

Why not try a different variety of biscuit base, such as ginger nuts mixed with digestives?

SERVES 6
150 g (5 oz) digestive biscuits, crushed
50 g (2 oz) melted butter
grated rind and juice of 2 limes
2 eggs
1 x 450 g (1 lb) can of condensed milk
icing sugar for dusting
whipped cream to serve

Pre-heat the oven to gas mark 4, 180°C (350°F). Mix together the biscuit crumbs and melted butter, then press into the base of a 20 cm (8 in) loose-bottomed pie dish or cake tin.
Whisk together the lime rind and juice, eggs and condensed milk and pour into the dish. Bake for 20–30 minutes until set. Dust with icing sugar, cut into wedges and serve warm or cold with whipped cream.

CREAMY COOL
Campari jellies

These little jellies have a wonderful bittersweet flavour and always prove very popular with those who don't really have a sweet tooth.

SERVES 4
1 x 135 g (4³/4 oz) packet tangerine or orange jelly
300 ml (10 fl oz) boiling water
1 x 150 ml (5 fl oz) carton double cream
4 tablespoons Campari
seeds and pulp of 4 passionfruit

Dissolve the jelly in the water. Stir well, then set aside to cool.
When cool, but before the jelly sets, stir in the cream, Campari and passionfruit. Pour into 4 small glasses and leave to set in the fridge.

MIDNIGHT MANGO
granita

Because mangoes have a such a lovely flavour of their own,
I've kept this very simple. Granitas are really easy to make and
are so refreshing – the perfect finish to any barbecue. Midnight
or midday, the choice is yours.

SERVES 8
1 lb (450 g) diced mango flesh
150 g (5 oz) caster sugar
600 ml (1 pint) cold water
juice of 1 lemon

Place the mango flesh in a liquidizer and whizz to make a
smooth purée. Add the caster sugar and whizz again, then, with
the motor running, pour in the water and the lemon juice.
Pour the mixture into a freezer-proof container and freeze for
2 hours. Break the crystals up with a fork, then return to the
freezer for at least another couple of hours.
If you plan to make this more than a few hours ahead, transfer
the granita to the fridge for 30 minutes before serving, then
break the crystals up with a fork and pile into pretty glasses.

Right: Midnight mango granitas

SUMMERY SOFT DRINKS

WATERMELON
and tarragon ice

This is a great drink to prepare ahead: simply freeze the watermelon and store the syrup in the fridge for up to five days, until ready to whizz together and serve. Don't forget to save the watermelon rinds so you can make the juicy pickle on page 19.

SERVES 4
400 g (14 oz) watermelon flesh, seeded and diced
200 ml (7 fl oz) water
25 g (1 oz) caster sugar
2 sprigs of fresh tarragon
juice of 1 lime

Freeze the melon dice for at least 4 hours, or overnight.

Place the water, sugar and tarragon in a small pan and gently bring to the boil, stirring occasionally, until the sugar dissolves. Remove from the heat and allow to cool completely. Strain into a small jug and chill.

Place the frozen watermelon in a food processor, switch on, and while it is running, pour in the syrup until the mixture forms a lovely slush. Add lime juice to taste and serve in tall glasses with straws for sucking up the crystals.

ROSEMARY LIMEADE

This is a zingy and refreshing long drink – ideal for cooling down on a summer's day. Rosemary has lots of medicinal properties but is also a great flavouring ingredient, especially in my wonderful limeade.

SERVES 4
150 ml (5 fl oz) water
50 g (2 oz) caster sugar
4 sprigs fresh rosemary
juice of 4 limes

TO SERVE
ice
lime twists
600 ml (1 pint) soda water

Place the water, sugar and rosemary in a small pan and gently bring to the boil, stirring, until the sugar dissolves. Remove from the heat and allow to cool completely. Strain into a small jug, stir in the lime juice, then chill until ready to serve.

Pack 4 tall glasses with ice, then pour over the rosemary and lime syrup. Top with the soda and decorate each glass with a twist of lime.

BETTY'S BRILLIANT
banana malt

A truly delicious and nutritious drink which is a real breakfast treat. If you can't get malt extract in your local supermarket, try a good health food shop or chemist. I buy mine at Betty's, hence the name.

SERVES 1
1 banana
150 ml (5 fl oz) ice-cold milk
1 teaspoon malt extract
ground nutmeg for dusting

Break the banana into a liquidizer or food processor and whizz until it forms a purée. With the motor running, slowly pour in the milk.
Turn off the blender, add the malt extract, then whizz again for several seconds until the mixture is thick and frothy. Pour into a large glass, dust with nutmeg and drink immediately.

DELICIOUS FROZEN
fruit cooler

This chillingly refreshing drink is quick and easy to make and because the fruit is frozen, you won't need to add any ice.

SERVES 6
250 g (9 oz) frozen summer fruits
1 tablespoon caster sugar

TO SERVE
lemonade
6 fresh mint leaves, shredded

Place the frozen summer fruit and the sugar in a food processor and whizz until finely minced. Pass through a fine sieve to remove any pips.
Pour the fruit purée equally into 6 tall chilled glasses. Slowly top up with lemonade, then add a sprinkling of fresh mint to each glass and serve. A bendy straw or two adds a nice finishing touch.

ROCK AND WHIZZ
papaya smoothie

Smoothies are so simple, and if you choose ripe, sweet fruit, you won't need to add extra sugar. This one is based on an Indian-style mango lassi, so I've added a pinch of salt. In Brazil I made one just like this using juicy local mangoes – scrummy.

SERVES 2
1 papaya or mango, skinned, seeded and diced
1 x 150 g (5 oz) carton natural yogurt
200 ml (7 fl oz) cold water
$1/4$ teaspoon salt
ice cubes to serve

Place the fruit in a food processor or liquidizer and whizz until puréed. Add the yogurt, water and salt and whizz until well blended.
Fill a tall tumbler with ice, pour over the smoothie and serve.

Below: I've just seen Elvis out jogging in his blue suede shoes. Who's laughing now, eh?

Right: Rock and whizz papaya smoothie, front Rosemary limeade, back (page 158) and Watermelon and tarragon ice, right (page 158)

COCKTAILS

'WHAT'S NEW,
pussycat?' strawberry daiquiri

Ernest Hemingway was famous for his novels, his love of pussycats and the odd one or two Cuban frozen cocktails, especially the daiquiri. When I was filming in the Florida Keys, his home for many years, I whizzed up a quick daiquiri using plump strawberries and fresh key limes. And here's that recipe – a real knock-out Ernest cool concoction! I'm sure my mate Tom Jones would also approve. Cheers!

SERVES 2
75 g (3 oz) fresh strawberries
1 teaspoon caster sugar
4 tablespoons white rum
juice of 1 lime
a glass of crushed ice

Place the strawberries and sugar in a blender and whizz briefly until pureéd. Add the rum, lime juice and crushed ice and whizz again until smooth. Pour into 2 champagne flutes, add straws and slip a sliced plump strawberry on to the rim of each flute. Serve accompanied by a good Hemingway novel, and the day just drifts away. Hmm...

REAL LONG ISLAND
iced tea

A traditional Long Island iced tea is a potent force and this recipe doesn't fail to deliver... Did someone say 'tea'? Not on your nelly!

SERVES 2
ice
2 tablespoons tequila
2 tablespoons rum
2 tablespoons vodka
2 tablespoons gin
2 tablespoons orange-based liqueur,
    such as Triple Sec or Cointreau
juice of 1 lemon
cola

Fill 2 tall glasses with ice and add a tablespoon of each spirit and the liqueur to each glass. Stir in the lemon juice, then top up with cola.

TENNESSEE
gold ice

I like to use a proper Tennessee sour-mash whiskey, such as Jack Daniels, for this drink, but you can use any bourbon or good-quality whiskey. For that ice-frosted look, stick your tumblers in the freezer a few hours before.

SERVES 1
ice
2 tablespoons whiskey
1 tablespoon dry sherry
juice of 1 large orange
soda water

Fill a tumbler with ice, then stir in the whiskey, sherry and orange juice. Top up with soda water and serve.

MISSISSIPPI WIGGLE
swizzle punch

This punch really gives you that wiggle swizzle appeal. Remember to remove the peel from the lemon before you squeeze out the juice.

SERVES 6
150 ml (5 fl oz) Southern Comfort
2 tablespoons brandy
juice of 1 lemon
1 teaspoon sugar
lemonade
ice and lemon-peel twists to serve

Fill a large jug with ice then add the Southern Comfort, brandy, lemon juice and sugar. Give it a quick swizzle.
Top the jug up with lemonade, decorate with a few lemon-peel twists and serve. After a few of these you'll be ready to wiggle away.

SCHMOOZY
manhattan

This classic American cocktail is one of my all-time favourites.

SERVES 1
2 tablespoons rye whiskey
1 tablespoon sweet vermouth
dash of Angostura bitters
1 cocktail cherry and cracked ice to serve

Mix together the whiskey, vermouth and bitters and pour into a short, ice-filled tumbler. Top with a cocktail cherry and serve.

COOL FROSTED
Atlantic jewel

This is a cross between a Margarita and a Sea Breeze. It's a really cool, refreshing long drink to kick your barbecue party off with a bang! I like to use sugar-frosted cocktail glasses: simply dip the rims first into beaten egg white and then into caster sugar.

SERVES 2
4 tablespoons tequila
2 tablespoons orange-based liqueur, such as Cointreau or Grand Marnier
400 ml (14 fl oz) cranberry juice
juice of 1 lime
cracked iced to serve

Mix together the tequila, orange liqueur, cranberry juice and lime juice.
Pour into 2 sugar-frosted, ice-filled glasses and serve.

CAIPIRIHNA

This is the national drink of Brazil – it's a lively 'stir and serve' cocktail made from *cachaca*, a white spirit distilled from sugar cane. I shook up a few of these while in Rio and they went down a treat. Made with vodka, it's called a *caipiroska*.

SERVES 1
1 small lime, cut into six wedges
1–2 tablespoons caster sugar
3–4 tablespoons cachaca
ice, to serve

Place the lime wedges and sugar in a strong glass tumbler and mash roughly with a wooden pestle or the end of a slim rolling pin. Add the spirit and ice, stir well and serve.

THEMED BARBECUE MENUS

Here are a few suggestions of dishes you could include if you wish to give a themed barbecue.

VEGETARIAN BARBECUE

A host of delicious veggie dishes – choose from starters,
main courses, side dishes, desserts and drinks.

Crispy spring rolls on the coals (page 43)
Molten taleggio fondue (page 36)
—

Smoked aubergine, tomato and basil
cannellini pasta (page 115)
Avocado cone quesadillas (page 118)
Artichokes Niçoise (page 119)
Oozing Oriental stuffed aubergine slices (page 112)
Fire-toasted tofu satay (page 114)
Brilliant barbie butter bean burgers (page 94)
—

Chomping caponata (page 123)
Cheese and bubble squeaky hotcakes (page 127)
Flamed polenta chips (page 135)
with Crumbly blue cheese mayonnaise (page 18)
—

Merida orange sunset caramels (page 154)
Papos Brazilian babas (page 152)
—

Watermelon and tarragon ice (page 158)
Real Long Island iced tea (page 162)

DINNER PARTY

For that special occasion, impress your friends
with these succulent first courses, mains,
accompaniments, desserts and drinks.

Parma fired figs with goats' cheese filling (page 35)
Succulent seared scallops with coriander and
garlic oil dressing (page 32)

—

Chilli-skin garlic-stuffed poussins (Oaxaca style) (page 47)
Jim's fire-glazed duck with fresh plum dipping sauce (page 56)
Chilli and mustard-crusted leg of lamb (page 58)
Charles Part's river eel with potacado salad (page 106)
Charred couscous pepper cups (page 114)

—

Garlic herb-tucked and tossed tomatoes (page 123)
Fiery chilli broccoli sticks (page 127)
Syd's chicory, blue cheese and walnut salad (page 132)
Baked garlic and fennel flatbread (page 143)

—

Midnight mango granita (page 156)

—

Delicious frozen fruit cooler (page 159)
Cool frosted Atlantic jewel (page 163)

BARBIE BRUNCH

Quick and easy brunch dishes, including a naughty dessert and a refreshing soft drink.

Barbie brunch or breakfast (page 30)
Mounties' Canadian pancakes (page 31)
Pulled pork sandwiches (page 78)
Speedy cheesy cornzales parcels (page 116)
Bubbling pesto mushroom cups (page 124)
Ranch-style pit baked beans (page 130)
Slap hand Brazilian cheese buns (page 139)
Chester's corn cakes (page 138)

—

Oaxaca chocolata omeletta (page 148)

—

Rock and whizz papaya smoothie (page 160)

Where barbecued food really comes alive – on the streets of Key West in Florida. This lot can't wait to get stuck in.

BUFFET PARTY

This tasty finger food will make your
buffet party go with a swing.

Mexican oyster shooters (page 34)
Molten taleggio fondue (page 36)
Jalapeño chilli-prawn ladders (page 42)
Dodg'em and down'em cowboy ribs (page 66)
Crispy chicken-thigh brochettes (page 54)
Spiced Mazatlán meatballs (page 60)
Ellen's Chicago deli pizza (page 140)
Aromatic charred bruschetta (page 136)
Wicked kicking salsa (page 16)
Alan and Andy's Amazonian fish kebabs (page 102)
Charred tasty tatties (page 122)
Scrumptious snap carrot salad (page 135)
—
Honeypone blueberry shortcakes (page 150)
Kharm Key lime pie (page 155)
—
Rosemary limeade (page 158)
Mississippi wiggle swizzle punch (page 163)

KID'S FEAST

Kids will love these barbecued treats, especially
the sweet and sticky puddings and malted milk shake.

Fire-fist chorizo quesadillas (page 79)
Moo pops sticky finger drumsticks (page 54)
Reuben's favourite fajitas burritos (page 82)
The giant kiddy beef burger (page 94)
Double dip spicy chips (page 126)
Spicy lime-charred corn on the cob (page 122)
Twice-baked hot-coal potatoes (page 126)
Crazy crunchy crispy coleslaw (page 132)

—

K.S.C. filo refuellers with toffee mud sauce (page 147)
Maple fire fruitbread pudding (page 151)

—

Betty's brilliant banana malt (page 159)

FOUR SIMPLE SUPPERS

Don't just limit your barbecues to parties –
here are some simple supper menus to cook
on a balmy summer evening.

Alabama chicken Brummie balti (page 48)
Table-top naans (page 139)
Midnight mango granita (page 156)

Salmon butter pit-pocket knots (page 96)
Garlic herb-tucked and tossed tomatoes (page 123)
Twice-baked hot-coal potatoes (page 126)

Oozing Osorio stuffed lamb (page 58)
Saffron-scented rice (page 130)
Fiery chilli broccoli sticks (page 127)

Crispy spring rolls on the coals (page 43)
Clare's Chinese crispy bubbled belly pork (page 72)
Stir-fried udon noodles (page 131)

Cool frosted Atlantic jewel (page 163)

BARBECUE INFORMATION

Whether you are an occasional or a regular barbecuer, there is a wide variety of barbecues to choose from, ranging from the small disposable trays to the most sophisticated grills set in glamorous trolleys with table attachments and all the gadgets. Here are some hints and guidelines on what to look out for.

WHICH TYPE OF BARBECUE DO YOU CHOOSE?

There are two basic types of barbecue available – charcoal or gas – and whichever type you choose, they both work on the same basic principles.

The food is placed on a rack over the heat and, as it cooks, it releases melted fat and cooking juices. These fall off on to the heat source (charcoal, coals, lava rocks or metal bars or plates), which converts this moisture into smoke that then rises up and flavours the food. Contrary to popular belief, charcoal in itself imparts no actual flavour – it is only the smoke from the cooking juices and any aromatics added to the coals that actually add any flavour to the food – so you do, in fact, get that same outdoor flavour when you use gas too.

THINGS TO LOOK OUT FOR WHEN BUYING A BARBECUE

GENERAL POINTS

Buy your barbecue from a well-known, trusted manufacturer who offers a good warranty, as well as replacement parts and accesories.

Choose a barbecue appropriate to your needs, depending on whether you barbecue just once or twice a year or regularly throughout the summer, and even winter. Also, if you wish to take your barbecue out and about with you – to the beach, on a picnic or when you go camping – buy one that is compact and easy to transport.

Take storage space for a dormant barbecue into account. Some of the larger ones will require garage or shed space when not in use.

Buy a barbecue that is made to last and that will withstand corrosion and remain rust-free. The more expensive ones will be better made and will last up to five times longer than the cheaper models.

Take the assembly of your new barbecue into account. Ask your dealer how easy or difficult it is to put together and roughly how long assembly will take: obviously, the more elaborate your barbecue, the more parts it will have, so clear, precise instructions are essential. Also check that the parts are precision-made so that they fit together well and easily, and make sure that there are no sharp, unrolled edges anywhere.

Check out the stability of the assembled barbecue because this is a very important safety aspect. Are the legs in proportion to the size of the hearth and thick and sturdy enough to withstand the weight of the barbecue once it is laden with hot coals and food? Also, will it be sturdy and wobble-free once in use? If the barbecue is set in a trolley with wheels, are they rugged enough to withstand the weight of the barbecue when moving it into position?

Choose a barbecue that offers you adequate primary cooking space for the number of people you wish to cater for on a regular basis. This means the actual cooking area over the coals rather than additional racks or warming shelves. Extra square inches overall do not always provide more cooking space. Those barbecues with stacked grills and warming racks may seem convenient and offer lots more space but they are often lacking when it comes to the practicalities of cooking.

Make sure that the cooking racks are in proportion to the size of the cooking area and are sturdy enough so that they do not sag under the weight of the food that the area can accommodate. Also check that the bars are not spaced too far apart or your food will be forever falling down between them. Slightly thicker bars will also sear a larger area of the food, giving it a more 'barbecued' flavour. Some racks are porcelain-enamelled, which will prevent the food sticking during cooking and prevent rusting when not in use, but they are a little heavier and may get chipped if you don't look after them.

The handles on any barbecue should be made of wood or cool-to-the-touch plastic, not metal. If you would like the option of cooking large joints of meat on your barbecue, choose one with a lid that is large enough to accommodate a joint.

With the fancier models, make sure that the table attachments are easy to clean, as well as heat- and weather-resistant.

CHARCOAL BARBECUES

There are those people who enjoy the fun of this more primitive, traditional style of cooking, which involves the hands-on activity of building and regulating a natural fire – you little cave person, you!

There is a wider price range of charcoal barbecues available, from the very cheap disposable trays to the more sophisticated models, as well as a bigger range of small or portable barbecues that enable you to cook in restricted spaces, such as on balconies and in small gardens, or while at the beach, camping, on holiday and so forth. If you choose to cook on charcoal, you have the option of constructing a barbecue yourself (from bricks or rocks and a rack) wherever and whenever you wish.

If buying a cast-iron barbecue, buy one made from virgin, solid cast iron. These have the ability to reach and withstand higher temperatures, diffuse heat more evenly and efficiently and retain heat for longer. Recycled cast iron contains impurities, bubbles and cracks, which might not withstand such high temperatures and could prove dangerous.

If you opt for a steel barbecue, buy one made from heavy-gauge steel sealed with porcelain enamel, which will be able to withstand the high cooking temperatures and make it easier to clean up afterwards.

Choose between an open rack or a covered grill. A grill with a hood will offer you more options on how the food can be cooked, but make sure there are enough air vents to allow maximum air flow. About three in the base and one in the lid is ideal.

Select a barbecue that is easy to clean for its size. Tipping the ashes out of a small, portable barbecue should pose no problems, but this would be far more difficult with the much larger models. Specially designed ash collectors in some barbecues make life much easier.

GAS BARBECUES

These grills are convenient and ready for use at the drop of a hat. They light at the touch of a button and are ready to cook on in about 10 minutes – much faster than charcoal. You also have better control over the temperature of your barbecue with gas. These barbecues are relatively inexpensive, easy to use and quick to clean up and store away after use.

Try to avoid barbecues with glass windows in the lid if you can. They serve no purpose, blacken very quickly and are very hard to clean. When the lids are closed, they tend to reflect the heat unevenly and can sometimes shatter under high temperatures.

Check that the gas burners in the base of the hearth are made from stainless steel, not aluminized steel. An H-shaped burner will give you more heat coverage. They also need to be shielded from the drippings so that they do not become clogged up during use. Individual controls for each burner will offer you more versatility, enabling you to cook by the direct or indirect method of cooking (see page 182).

Make sure that it is easy to connect and remove the gas tanks before and after use. An accurate gauge indicating the level of fuel in the tank is useful so that it doesn't run out during cooking. A rubber connecting hose is also more durable and efficient than a plastic one.

Check out the type and location of the ignition systems. A convenient, easy-to-use push-button system makes life a lot easier.

Ask questions about the fuel consumption of gas barbecues. Some models claim to have good heat outputs, but when you use them, go through a tank of gas like it's going out of fashion. Look out for one with the most efficient system.

Overleaf: I don't know why, but this mountain of dried pimentos in the Mercado Juarez, Mexico, has got me all excited. Look at the size of it!

THE TYPES OF CHARCOAL AND GAS BARBECUES AVAILABLE

CHARCOAL BARBECUES

Disposable barbecues

These are now readily available in most DIY shops, supermarkets and department stores, especially during the summer months. They consist of shallow foil trays filled with charcoal and a sheet of firelighting paper.

They are cheap and portable, ideal for small spaces, especially balconies, and are very easy to light. The only disadvantages are that they do not offer much primary cooking area (although they do stay hot for an amazingly long time, so you could cook food in rotation if you wished) and the rack is very close to the coals, which means that they are only really suitable for cooking small, thin pieces of food such as burgers, chops, sausages and kebabs. Larger, thicker pieces of food would blacken too much on the outside before being properly cooked in the middle.

Disposable barbecues can be set on the ground or placed at table-top height on a heat-resistant surface.

Hibachi barbecues

These are shallow, trough-like, portable barbecues, originating from Japan, which stand on very short legs and can be set on the ground or on a heat-resistant surface at table-top height. They have two vertical, notched rungs set on one long side of the hearth into which the cooking rack can be locked, enabling you to adjust the distance of the foods from the coals, depending on the cooking time required. These are not really suitable for cooking very large joints of meat.

Convertible barbecues

These simple, portable, cast-iron barbecues have an L-shaped hearth that can be used in the traditional way, with the hot coals sitting beneath the horizontal cooking rack. However, they can also be rotated by 90° so that the coals produce a vertical back-burner in front of which a spike can be positioned for spit roasting. They can be positioned either on the ground or at table-top height.

Upright open-top barbecues

These come in all shapes and sizes and simply consist of an open hearth without a lid, either supported on legs or set into a simple trolley with wheels. Once they are assembled, they require somewhere for storage when not in use. Plastic covers are available, but do not really offer long-term protection. This type of barbecue can be used only for the direct method of cooking and offer no protection from strong winds.

Barrel barbecues

These look like little pot-bellied stoves and offer a very attractive, stable, open-top style barbecue at table-top height. They are made from cast iron, have adjustable cooking racks and, often, stands for accommodating rotisserie spits. The main advantage is that their unique design makes them very easy to light and quick to reach cooking temperature, unlike most other charcoal barbecues, which can take up to 45 minutes to heat up properly. Newspaper or kindling is placed underneath the charcoal grate, which is then replaced and covered with the charcoal. The air vent in the side of the barbecue is opened and the kindling or newspaper is lit, which ignites the charcoal so quickly that is ready to cook on in just 10–15 minutes.

Pillar or pedestal barbecues

These consist of a hearth set on a thick tube-like pedestal and work in a similar way to the barrel barbecues. The pillar is packed with newspaper and the coals are arranged in the hearth above. The paper, which quickly lights the barbecue above, is lit with a taper via a hole in the pillar.

Covered kettle barbecues

These come in various sizes, offering a range of primary cooking areas, as well as other accessories such as ash catchers, various cleaning systems and built-in thermometers. There are small, portable barbecues, which are ideal for picnics and balconies, free-standing models, and versions that are mounted in trolleys with added extras such as fuel-storage bins and gas-ignition systems. Not only can they be used for the more traditional direct method of cooking (see page 182) – as with an open-top barbecue – but they also have rounded lids, meaning you can cook by the indirect method (see page 182), which allows them to act like conventional ovens when the lid is closed. The heat from the coals is reflected evenly around the foods, reducing the cooking times, sealing in the juices and enhancing that smoky 'barbecue' flavour. This method also removes oxygen from the cooking surface, eliminating the possibility of flare-ups, which are caused when the fatty cooking juices fall into the fire.

Hooded barbecues

These are generally large, rectangular barbecues with hinged lids set into movable trolleys. They work in the same way as kettle barbecues and are often available with extras such as movable grates, rotisseries, warming racks, side tables, separate burners for side dishes and so on.

Permanent brick barbecues

Some companies now offer do-it-yourself kits to construct permanent barbecues in your garden. Strong metal pegs mounted in a three-sided brick wall support a solid plate for the coals and a large metal rack above. These are ideal for people who do a lot of barbecuing because they provide lots of primary cooking space and they are always available for use whenever the mood takes you.

GAS BARBECUES
Portable barbecues

These can be small, round or rectangular hooded barbecues, with short legs that sometimes swing up and over the lid to lock it in place during transport. They run on small, disposable gas cylinders that heat either lava rocks or flat flavourizing bars or plates. They are ideal for picnics, beach parties and camping holidays and for people with limited storage space who like to do a little barbecuing every now and then.

Table-height barbecues

These are always set into table-height trolley units usually with wheels, which means that they can be easily manoeuvred into place before use. They range from the most simple of trolleys with one small side table, right up to those with half the cooking area given over to a solid griddle plate, rotisseries, thermometers, smoker units, baking ovens, racks for holding cooking oils and sauces, enclosed shelved cupboards below and side-burners for side dishes and sauces.

ELECTRIC BARBECUES

These barbecues are available in small table-top sizes or larger table-height models and are heated by an electric element positioned under the rack. They

act something like a domestic grill in reverse (with the heat coming from underneath). Their main disadvantage is that they need to be used near a power point or connected to a long extension lead.

FUELS

The secret to a good barbecue is a good fire. The art of achieving this, controlling the heat and distributing it evenly comes with practice, but you will need the right fuel before you can begin.

WOOD

Dry hardwood can be used for barbecuing foods, but it is more difficult to start and the fire will not last as long as either charcoal or briquettes. Wood is best for hand-built, impromptu barbecues.

CHARCOAL

Lumpwood charcoal and charcoal briquettes are the two main types of fuel for a charcoal barbecue.

Lumpwood charcoal

This is not a fossil fuel extracted from the ground as some people would believe, but is, in fact, wood that has been fired in a kiln. This process cooks the wood without igniting it and drives out all the by-products, leaving behind a very light, black, combustible form of carbon.

Good-quality charcoal pieces are normally fairly large, making barbecuing much easier.

The 'green issue'

The increasing popularity of barbecuing means that the demand on the world's forests is increasing. In the past few years, charcoal production has been a contributing factor to the deforestation of the tropical rainforests because it has been unregulated, but now an international organization called the Forest Stewardship Council (FSC), sponsored by the Worldwide Fund for Nature, has been set up to monitor and regulate the use of trees from selected areas of forests. Charcoal with the FSC logo is now available in most of the UK's large retail outlets.

Instant-lighting lumpwood charcoal

This is a very convenient form of charcoal which has been impregnated with a lighting agent. About 1 kg (2 $^1/_4$ lb) of fuel is sold in a sealed paper bag which is simply placed in the hearth and then lit with a match, therefore removing the need for firelighters or lighting fluids. Once this charcoal is alight, more fuel can be added to the hearth if necessary to give you a bigger bed of coals.

Charcoal briquettes
These are uniformly shaped lumps of fuel made from particles of waste charcoal mixed with a starch binder. Once lit, these tend to burn for longer than lumpwood charcoal.

Other barbecue fuels
Some cheap barbecue briquettes are made from alternative sources of fuel, filled out with things such as sand, sawdust and anthracite, all bound together with a petroleum-based substance. For good, 'natural' barbecuing, it is better to choose a quality briquette made from pure lumpwood charcoal.

GAS
Barbecues fuelled by gas can be run on either Liquid Petroleum (LP) gas or natural gas. LP gas is available in two forms: butane, which generally comes in a blue cylinder, or propane, which comes in a red cylinder. It is best to use propane gas in cold weather as it operates at a lower temperature than butane. Natural gas is not available in Europe in cylinder form. Special fittings which can be attached to the outside wall of the house will draw gas from the main supply and can be connected to the barbecue when required. The disadvantage with this system is that the barbecue needs to be used close to the house.

FIRELIGHTERS

There are a number of different ways of lighting a charcoal barbecue.

Barbecue firelighters
These waxy-looking cubes or sticks are specially designed to light barbecues without giving off any fumes that will taint the food. A recommended number are simply pushed in among the charcoal or briquettes and then lit with a match. As they stay alight for quite a few minutes, they give time for the charcoal to ignite. They are also clean, very safe and easy to use. It is important not to use other types of firelighters, which are designed for lighting indoor

domestic fires. These contain paraffin, which could badly taint the food.

Firelighter fluid
This is a commonly used product for lighting a barbecue as it is odourless, clean and safe in the proper hands. However, it is very dangerous if used incorrectly and should never be squirted directly on to a burning fire as the flame could travel back up to the bottle in a split second. Pour a little of the firelighter fluid on to the dry fuel and leave it to soak in for 2–3 minutes. Then light it with a taper or long safety match.

Firelighter gels
These thick, sticky gels are squeezed on to the dry fuel and then set alight. However, great care must be taken not to get them on the fingers in case they catch alight when you go to ignite the barbecue, which could result in a nasty burn.

Electric starters
These are flat, looped heating elements attached to a handle and an electric cable. They are placed in among the coals, switched on and left until the coals catch fire. The disadvantage is that you will need an electric power point nearby.

FIRE AROMATICS

Barbecued foods can be given a more distinctive flavour by adding either natural or manufactured flavourings to the fire just before cooking.
- Dry twigs from fruit trees and vine cuttings can be added to a charcoal barbecue.
- The woody stalks and leaves of some fresh herbs, such as rosemary, thyme or bay, can be added to a charcoal barbecue.
- Left-over almond, walnut and hazelnut shells which have been soaked in water for 30 minutes can be sprinkled on to a charcoal barbecue.
- Soaked dried seaweed can be added to a charcoal barbecue when cooking fish and shellfish.

My kinda place – lots of great-tasting, home-made icecream and other goodies in the Mercado Juarez, Oaxaca, Mexico

■ Small chips, made from old whisky barrels or hickory, mesquite, oak, apple or plum wood can be used on either charcoal or gas barbecues. The loose chips should be soaked in cold water for 30 minutes beforehand and can be sprinkled directly on to a charcoal barbecue just before cooking. For gas barbecues they should be rolled up into a foil sausage, pierced here and there with a skewer and then rested on the lava rocks or flavourizer bars.

SMOKERS

Smoking food cooks it very slowly, while giving it a full flavour. Various types of smokers are available.

WATER SMOKERS
Traditional smokers are fired by charcoal, which is topped with green or damp wood to produce the smoke that flavours the food. There is normally a basin of water set over the heat source, which creates a little steam and evens out the distribution of the smoke. The water means that meats tend not to dry out even after several hours' cooking. The gentle temperatures involved also make it possible to home smoke many different kinds of food, such as cheese and garlic, without actually cooking them. Owning a smoker is an opportunity for lots of wild experimentation.

The amount of smoke created is incredible, so you must have a large open space in which to cook. Do not attempt to use a water smoker on a balcony or in a small back yard in the way you could a portable barbecue.

Most barbecue stores stock a range of water smokers with their own operating instructions.

HOME SMOKERS
Many specialized cookshops and barbecue stores sell miniature home smokers. These very compact little devices use methylated spirits as a heat source and fine wood chippings to create the smoke. They don't usually have a thermometer, so you cannot monitor the temperature inside. While they cannot be used for large amounts of food, they are very good for smoking things such as sausages or fish. They're very portable and are ideal for taking away on trips or holidays.

Smoker fuel
The smoke flavour comes from the wood that you load into your equipment. It's very important that you use wood chips or chunks that are specifically for smoking. Wood from resinous trees, such as pine, will absolutely ruin the flavour of your food.

The wood you use must either be very young or wet in order to create the smoke – dry wood will simply burn. You can buy purpose-made wood chips, which should be soaked for an hour or so before using. Good ones to try include hickory, mesquite or wood from fruit or nut trees such as peach or pecan.

GETTING THINGS READY

Place your barbecue on a level surface away from trees, fences, hedges, etc. If it is windy, try to find somewhere a bit more sheltered.

Allow at least 45 minutes for a charcoal barbecue to reach the correct cooking temperature. A gas barbecue is probably ready to cook on in about 10 minutes.

Remove any chilled meats from the fridge and allow them to come back to room temperature.

Make sure that everything else is ready so that once the barbecue has reached the right temperature, you can start cooking and serve up straight away.

COOKING ON A CHARCOAL BARBECUE

LIGHTING THE BARBECUE
Do not be tempted to fill the hearth with charcoal in the hope of making a fire that will last longer and cook better. It is simply a waste of fuel and the fire will become too hot to cook on anyway.

Remove the lid, if there is one, and open all the vents. Spread the charcoal or briquettes two layers deep over the base of the barbecue. Scoop it back up into a pyramid and tuck in the firelighters, if you are using any.

Light the firelighters and leave until the coals start to glow red (5–10 minutes). Rake the coals back out into an even layer and leave until they have reached the required temperature (30–45 minutes).

COOKING TEMPERATURES

Hot

The flames will have disappeared and coals will be glowing red and covered with a light dusting of white ash. You should be able to hold your hand about 15 cm (6 in) away from the coals for about 2 seconds maximum. This temperature is suitable only for very thin pieces of food, such as chicken escalopes, fish fillets and chipolata sausages.

Medium hot

The coals should now be covered with a thicker layer of white ash and you should be able to hold your hand above the fire for about 5 seconds.

This temperature is suitable for most food cooked on the barbecue.

Cool

The coals will no longer be glowing red and will be covered in a very thick layer of ash. You should be able to hold your hand over the fire for about 8 seconds. This temperature is fine for foods, such as fresh fruit parcels, that simply need warming through rather than cooking.

You can also alter the way the food is cooked by moving it closer to or further away from the heat (obviously, the closer it is, the more heat it will be subjected to and vice versa). You will find that food placed directly over the coals will get hotter than food pushed to the side of the rack away from the hottest part of the fire.

Regulating the temperature

To increase the temperature of the fire a little, knock some of the ash off the coals and push them a little closer together.

To cool the barbecue down, spread out the coals a little and partly close any vents.

If you need to cook on the barbecue for any more than 45 minutes to 1 hour, you will need to add more coals. Either push the coals together and add new ones around the edge or, alternatively, light a new batch of coals in a second barbecue or a large metal roasting tin as soon as the first lot is ready and transfer them to the cooling fire with metal tongs.

METHODS OF COOKING

DIRECT COOKING

Direct cooking means that the food is placed on a rack directly over a solid area of heat (a bed of hot coals or a gas burner). The barbecue can be used uncovered or covered. The foods need to be turned so that both sides become cooked: they can be seared over the hottest part of the fire in the centre of the rack and then moved to the edge to finish cooking through. This method is ideal for cooking things that require up to 45 minutes' cooking time.

INDIRECT COOKING

This means that the heat source is restricted to the edges of the hearth, leaving a space clear in the centre for the food and a drip tray. Indirect cooking is possible only on a lidded barbecue. With charcoal barbecues the coals are placed on opposite sides of the hearth, while on gas barbecues with dual burners the middle burner closest to the food is turned off. The food is placed on the rack directly above the drip tray and then the lid is lowered into place. Since heat is reflected off the lid as well as coming from underneath, the barbecue acts almost like a conventional oven, which means that the food doesn't need to be turned during cooking. This method is ideal for cooking large joints of meat, such as whole chickens and legs of lamb. When using this method, try not to lift the lid too often because a lot of heat is lost this way. Add a little extra cooking time to compensate for each time you take a peek at the food.

SPIT ROASTING

Some charcoal and gas barbecues can accommodate spit-roasting attachments, or come with them already supplied. The meat is skewered on to the spit rod and held in place on either side with two adjustable spit forks. The rod is suspended over the heat (it is sometimes necessary to remove the rack first so that the food has enough room in which to turn) and the food is left to rotate slowly, powered either by a battery or an electrically driven motor.

SAFETY GUIDELINES

- Always read the manufacturer's instructions carefully before assembling and using a new barbecue.
- Always set a barbecue on a firm, level surface away from anything that could catch fire, such as fences, trees, hedges, etc.
- Always place portable barbecues on a heatproof surface or the ground.
- Never try to start a barbecue in high winds.
- Never use a barbecue indoors unless it has been specially designed for this purpose.
- Always open the lid of a gas barbecue before lighting.
- Once the barbecue is alight, never leave it unattended, and keep children and animals away from it.
- Never use charcoal on a gas barbecue. Charcoal burns very hot and in most cases will melt the shell of a gas barbecue. Also, charcoal burns to ash, which would mix with the cooking fats and clog up the gas burners.
- Never light a barbecue with paraffin, petrol or white spirit. Not only is this extremely dangerous, but it would also taint the food and render it inedible. Use only purpose-branded firelighters and fuels, and follow the manufacturer's instructions carefully.
- Keep matches well away from a lit barbecue.
- Never attempt to move a barbecue once lit.
- For gas barbecues, always check that the gas regulator is appropriate for the barbecue. Also check that the gas hose has not perished or cracked in any way and that it is properly connected to the barbecue and the gas cylinder before lighting.
- Dress sensibly when cooking on a barbecue. Try to avoid long, loose clothing and wear an apron to avoid burns from spitting fats, etc.
- Always leave a barbecue to cool down completely before cleaning it and packing it away. This can take several hours.
- Never try to extinguish a barbecue by pouring cold water on to it. There is the possibility that the metal hearth could contract and crack and porcellain-enamelled surfaces might shatter.

CLEANING UP A BARBECUE

CHARCOAL BARBECUES

Remove the cooking rack once cold and scrub off as much residue as you can with a wire brush or crumpled piece of foil. Then wash it with an abrasive, soap-filled scouring pad. It might be necessary to use an oven cleaner, too, every once in a while. If you look after the rack, it will give you better service for much longer.

Remove the cold ashes from the hearth and brush out the fine dust.

Occasionally, clean the rest of the barbecue with an oven cleaner to get rid of any accumulated greases and dirt. Rinse thoroughly and make sure it is completely dry before you pack it away.

GAS BARBECUES

Always clean the rack, lid, any drip trays, gas burners, etc. before packing it away.

Lava rocks can be cleaned a couple of times during their life to get rid of old cooking fats and juices. Wash them in hot soapy water, rinse and leave to dry. However, they do need to be replaced every now and then, otherwise old cooking juices can flavour the new food next time you use it.

Giving the outside of the barbecue a good wash with warm soapy water now and then keeps it looking nice and helps it to last longer.

Adios, everyone. Can I go home now?

BARBECUE EQUIPMENT

ESSENTIAL
- Long-handled tongs, spatulas and forks are essential for turning foods and removing them from the cooking rack.
- A long-handled basting brush is essential for brushing glazes on to partly cooked meats.
- Oven mitts are a must for removing kebabs, etc. from the barbecue.
- You will need an assortment of skewers. Long, flat metal skewers are ideal for chunky meat and fish kebabs and for holding spatchcocked poultry and butterflied joints of meat flat during cooking. Long and short bamboo skewers are ideal for small, more delicate foods that require shorter cooking times. Small, fine metal trussing skewers are great for sealing in stuffings and holding rolled foods together during cooking. Cocktail sticks will do a similar job.

NON-ESSENTIAL BUT USEFUL
- Hinged wire racks are available for barbecuing large individual fish, more than one small fish, sausages, burgers and kebabs, etc. They make it much easier and quicker to turn the food over during cooking and help to prevent it from sticking to the rack.
- Fine wire mesh racks that rest on the bars of the main cooking rack are useful for cooking small items of food which would otherwise fall through the bars.
- A wire brush and scraper make the job of cleaning up the cooking rack a lot easier and are also useful for quickly removing large pieces of stuck-on food from the rack during cooking.
- A meat thermometer will help you to test the internal temperature of large joints of meat.

OTHER POSSIBLE ATTACHMENTS AND ACCESSORIES
- Specially designed kebab racks enable you to suspend half a dozen skewers over the heat at once. As they do not come into contact with the rack during cooking, there is no problem with the kebabs sticking and they are also much easier to turn.
- Some barbecues enable you to attach a battery- or electrically-driven rotisserie, which is great for cooking whole chickens and large joints of meat.
- Plastic covers for both charcoal and gas barbecues will help protect them from dust and debris while they are in storage, and, in the short term, from the ravages of the weather outside.

BARBECUE SUPPLIERS

It is not always easy to know where to go to buy a barbecue or to find the specific barbecue that you are looking for.

- DIY stores, department stores and garden centres all stock barbecues and accessories, especially during the summer months.
- Supermarkets, particularly the larger superstores, stock a suprisingly wide range or barbecues, fuels and accessories.
- Petrol stations stock disposable barbecues, charcoal and firelighters, etc. during the summer months.
- Hardware stores and camping shops will stock the gas cylinders for a gas barbecue, and probably charcoal too.
- The Barbeque Shop at 46A Portsmouth Road, Cobham, Kent (01932 866 044) stocks a wide selection of charcoal and gas barbecues and operates a mail order service.
- Lakeland Ltd. (01539 488 100) supply portable barbecues and accessories by mail order.
- Special cookware shops usually carry a range of cooking accessories.
- British Gas Energy Centres supply gas barbecues. Freefone 0800 850 900 for details of your nearest store.

And here are a few numbers of barbecue manufacturers who will be able to give you the names and addresses of your nearest stockists:

Weber-Stephen Products Ltd. (charcoal and gas barbecues) (01462) 475 000

Landmann charcoal and gas barbecues (01299) 251 747/250 909

Black Knight barbecues (01622) 671 771/2

Odell charcoal and gas barbecues (01352) 762 061

Camping Gaz gas barbecues (0800) 317 466

INDEX

Page numbers in *italic* refer to the illustrations

ACKNOWLEDGEMENTS

A very special and warm-hearted thank you to Silvana Franco, whose attention to detail and commitment to the project were very much appreciated. Silvana showed immense creative flair, and her support and knowledge were exemplary. You're great, Vana!

To my other food stylist on location, Angela Boggiano, for her creativity, hard work and beautiful smile. And to all the crew; my directors Lynda Maher and Micci Billinger, producer Sara Kozak, cameraman Alan Duxbury, sound engineer Andy Morton, researcher extraordinaire Sue Ashcroft and of course Mr Fixit, Jim Hargreaves. They really brought the TV series alive. To my location photographer Craig Easton for capturing some magical moments.

To everyone at BBC Books who made the *Big Cook Out* happen beautifully. To Gus Filgate for his wonderful studio photography. My agent and friend Jeremy Hicks and the lovely Sarah Dalkin. My woman, wonderful wife and great mother Clare (sorry I've been away so much...). Our fabulous children Jimmy Roo and Madeleine Moo Pops – Daddy loves you. And, although he knows nothing, my adorable dog Oscar.

Thanks also to the following people who made our work on location so much easier and enjoyable:

Newfoundland: Environment Canada; Joe O'brien; Diana Parsons and the Department of Tourism; Quidi Vidi Brewery; Trapper John's; Gerald Smith; Steven and Pat Watson.

Western Quebec: 'A division' the Royal Canadian Mounted Police; Rachel Duplisea and the Canadian Museum of Civilisation; Jim Coffee; Pierre and Andree-Ann Crete; France Faucher and the Association Touristique de l'Outaouais; Andre Groulx and the Hull-Chelsea-Wakefield steam train; Dean Hamill; Paula Laing and Destination Quebec; Trudy Metcalfe; Charles Part and Jennifer Warren-Part; Remi and Sylvie Paul; Dennis Woods.

Kansas: Carolyn Wells and the Kansas City Barbecue Society; Bob Faulkner and the Benjamin Ranch; Maxine O'Dell, Kevin Pilgrim; Amazing Grace and the Grand Emporium; the Outlaws of Dodge City.

Chicago: Ellen Miller and friends, especially Norman Miller.

Memphis: Sharon Fox O'Guin and the Memphis Film Commission; Memphis Belle Memorial Association; the Peabody Hotel; Elvis Presley Enterprises, inc.; John Miller Charles Vergos and the Rendezvous.

Birmingham, Alabama: Amy Odum, Dilcy Hilley and the Birmingham Visitors and Convention Centre; Wayne Ellis and O.T's Sports Grill; the Whistle Stop Cafe.

Florida: Casa Alante, Cheryl and Rod Millar; NASA, Bill Johnson, Melissa Tomasso and Karen Kleinschmidt at Kennedy Space Centre.

Mexico: Peter Maxwell and the Camino Real Hotel, Oaxaca; Ileana and Ernesto de la Vega at El Naranjo.

Brazil: Gracas Fish, Nana and Tempero de Dada.

Argentina: Rene Griffiths.